First World War
and Army of Occupation
War Diary
France, Belgium and Germany

25 DIVISION
Divisional Troops
Divisional Ammunition Column
27 September 1915 - 31 March 1919

WO95/2234/4

The Naval & Military Press Ltd
www.nmarchive.com
Published in association with The National Archives

Published by

The Naval & Military Press Ltd

Unit 10 Ridgewood Industrial Park,

Uckfield, East Sussex,

TN22 5QE England

Tel: +44 (0) 1825 749494

www.naval-military-press.com

www.nmarchive.com

This diary has been reprinted in facsimile from the original. Any imperfections are inevitably reproduced and the quality may fall short of modern type and cartographic standards.

© **Crown Copyright**
Images reproduced by permission of The National Archives, London, England, 2015.

Contents

Document type	Place/Title	Date From	Date To
Heading	WO95/2234/4 Divisional Ammunition Column.		
Heading	25th Divl Ammn Column Sep 1915-Mar 1919		
Heading	25th Division 25th Divl A.C. Vol I Sept & Oct 15 Mar 19		
War Diary	Aldershot	27/09/1915	27/09/1915
War Diary	Southampton	27/09/1915	27/09/1915
War Diary	Havre	28/09/1915	28/09/1915
War Diary	En Route To Hazebrouck	29/09/1915	29/09/1915
War Diary	Hazebrouck	30/09/1915	30/09/1915
War Diary	St Jans Cappel	30/09/1915	04/10/1915
War Diary	St Jans Cappel & Point A.	05/10/1915	07/10/1915
War Diary	3 Section At St Jans Cappel Head Quarters 215 Miles NW Of Nieppe On Bailleul Nieppe Road Reference Map Hazebrouck Belgium 1/100000	08/10/1915	31/10/1915
Heading	25th Division 25th D.A.C. Vol 2 Nov 15		
War Diary	###	01/11/1915	30/11/1915
Heading	25th D.A.C. Vol 3		
War Diary	Headquarters On Bailleul Armentieres Near It Junction With Road Neuve Eglise Section Of The D.A.C. At St Jans Cappel Sheet 5A Hazebrouck Belgium 1/100000	01/12/1915	12/12/1915
War Diary	Headquarters & 3 Section At St Jans Cappel And Detachment At A Point On Bailleul Armentieres Road Near To Junction With Road Nr Neuve Eglise Sheet 5A Hazebrouck Belgium 1/100000	13/12/1915	31/12/1915
Heading	25th Divisional Ammunition Column January 1916		
War Diary	###	01/01/1916	16/01/1916
War Diary	Ammunition Depot At A Point About 100 East Of Junction Of Bailleul Nieppe & Steenwerck Neuve Eglise Roads	17/01/1916	31/01/1916
Heading	25th Divisional Ammunition Column February 1916		
War Diary	Headquarters & Section On Road Meteren Mont Noir Between La Manche On The North & Road Junction N Of H Of Fontaine Houck On The South Detachment Employed In Moory Road Malanal At The A Of La Creche 2 1/2 Miles S E Of Bailleul	01/02/1916	29/02/1916
Heading	25th Divisional Ammunition Column March 1916		
War Diary	Head Quarters & Min 2 & 3 Section On The Meteren Mont Noir Road N & S Of Schaexken 1 Kilometer W.N.W. Of St Jans Cappel No 1 Section At La Creche Sheet 5A Hazebrouck Belgium 1/100000	01/03/1916	07/03/1916
War Diary	Headquarters & 3 Section On Meteren Mont Noir Road N & S Of Schaexken 1 Kilometer W N Of St Jans Cappel	08/03/1916	11/03/1916
War Diary	H.Q. & 3 Section At Sains Les Pernes Sheet 11-Lens France 1/100000	12/03/1916	18/03/1916
War Diary	Head Quarters & No 1 Section At Maisnil St Pol No 2 Section At Ococche No 3 Section At Tachincourt Reference Map Sheet 11 Lens France 1/100000	19/03/1916	29/03/1916
War Diary	Maisnil St Pol	30/03/1916	31/03/1916
Heading	25th Divisional Ammunition Column April 1916		

War Diary	Headquarters & No 1 Section Maisnil St Pol No 2 2 Section Of Ocoche No 3 Section Les 1 Subsection At Tachincourt 1 Sub Section Of NW 3 Section At Berles Ref Sheet 1 W 11 France Lens France 1/10000	01/04/1916	21/04/1916
War Diary	Head Quarters & No 2 & 3 Section At Villers Brulin No 1 Section At Maisnil St Pol	22/04/1916	30/04/1916
Heading	25th Divisional Ammunition Column May 1916		
Miscellaneous	D.A.G. 3rd Echelon	03/06/1916	03/06/1916
War Diary	Head Quarters & No 1 Section At Villers Brulin No 2 & No 3 Section (Lens Detachment Of 1.0-38 O. R. 58 Hours At Ecroives Station 1 Officer 1 N.C.O-22 Gunners 5 Division At ACQ At Ecroives Reference Map 11 Lens France 1/100000	01/05/1916	20/05/1916
War Diary	No 1 Section Maisnil Nos 2 & 3 Section At Villers Brulin Headquarters & Ammn Dump at Le Pendu Reference Map No 11 Lens France 1/100000	21/05/1916	27/05/1916
War Diary	Head Quarters & No 4 Section Villers Brulin No 1 & 3 Section Cambligneul No 2 Section ACQ Ammunition Dump Le Pendu	28/05/1916	31/05/1916
Heading	25th Divisional Ammunition Column June 1916		
Miscellaneous	The Office In Change	01/07/1916	01/07/1916
War Diary	Head Quarters & No 1 2 3 & 4 Section At Cambligneul Ref Map No 11 Lens France 1/100000	01/06/1916	14/06/1916
War Diary	Headquarters 1 2 3 & 4 Section At Cambligneul Ref Map No 11 Lens France 1/100000	15/06/1916	28/06/1916
War Diary	H.Q. & 4 Section At Contay Map No 11 Lens France 1/100000	29/06/1916	30/06/1916
Heading	25th Division Ammunition Column July 1916		
War Diary	Headquarters & No 1 2 3 4 Section Of Contay Ref Map Lens France 1/100000	01/07/1916	04/07/1916
War Diary	H.Q. & A Echelon D.A.C. At Bouzincourt B Echelon At Warloy	05/07/1916	07/07/1916
War Diary	Bouzincourt	08/07/1916	25/07/1916
War Diary	S. A. N Section With Infantry At 25th Div	26/07/1916	31/07/1916
Heading	25th Divisional Ammunition Column August 1916		
War Diary	Bouzincourt Head Quarters 1 2 & 3 Central Per 4 Section Warloy Reference Map No 11 Lens France 1/100000	01/08/1916	08/08/1916
War Diary	Headquarters Ammunition Dump At No 1 & 2 Section Between Bouzincourt & Senlis No 3 Section Between Bouzincourt Millencourt No 4 Section At Warloy Reference Map No 11 Lens France 1/100000	09/08/1916	22/08/1916
War Diary	Dump Of Headquarters At V 3b10.5 Map 57D France 1/40000 On Hedauville Warloy Road No 1 2 & 3 Section On Same Road	23/08/1916	31/08/1916
Heading	25th. Division Ammunition Column. September 1916		
War Diary	V.4.a.0.5 On Hedauville Warloy Rd Map 57 D France 1/40000	01/09/1916	05/09/1916
War Diary	Headquarters & Dump As Above No 1 2 & 3 Section Adjutant On The Same Road No 4 Section At Warloy	06/09/1916	16/09/1916
War Diary	Headquarters 1 2 3 & 4 Section As Before	17/09/1916	30/09/1916
Heading	25th Divisional Ammunition Column October 1916		
War Diary	Headquarters 1 2 & 3 Section On Bouzincourt Albert Road Dump And W 20a7.5 Map 57.0 From 1/40000 4th Section At Warloy	01/10/1916	31/10/1916
Heading	25th Divisional Ammunition Column November 1916		

War Diary	Headquarters No 1 2 & 3 Section On Bouzincourt Albert Road Near Bouzincourt No 4 Section At Warloy Refernce Map No 11 Lens 1/100000	01/11/1916	26/11/1916
War Diary	Valhuon	27/11/1916	27/11/1916
War Diary	Ligny-Les-Aire	28/11/1916	28/11/1916
War Diary	Thiennes	29/11/1916	29/11/1916
War Diary	Le Roukloshill	30/11/1916	30/11/1916
Heading	25th Divisional Ammunition Column December 1916		
War Diary	Le Roukloshille Fienal Meteren Chessiler Map NE UA? Hazebrouck Belgium 1/100000	01/12/1916	17/12/1916
War Diary	Headquarters At B 9 C81 No 1 Section B23 C22 No 2 Section B14a63 No 3 Section B8b15 No 4 Section B14c96 Gum And Dump B11b20 Grenada Dump B5b37 Ref Map Sheet 36 N.W. France 1/20000	18/12/1916	31/12/1916
Miscellaneous	To D.A.G. G.H.Q. 3rd Echelon.	10/03/1917	10/03/1917
War Diary	Headquarters B9c81 No 1 Section B23c22 No 2 Section At B14a63 No 3 Section B8b15 No 4 Section At B14c96 Gun Ammn Dump At B11b20 Granade & S. A. A. Dump At B5b37 Ref Map Sheet 36 N. W. France 1/20000	01/01/1917	31/01/1917
War Diary	Headquarters B9c81 No 1 Section B23c22 No 2 Section Part At B14a63 Part At B23c53 No 3 Section B8b15 No 4 Section B14c96 Ref. France Sheet 36 N. W. Sect 1/20000 Gun Ammn Dump B11b20 Grenade & 5a.a. Dump B5b37	01/02/1917	12/02/1917
War Diary	Headquarters B.9c.81	13/02/1917	28/02/1917
War Diary	Headquarters No 1 2 & 3 Sections At Setques (B) (4) Map Sheet 5.a. Hazebrouck Belgium 1/100000	01/03/1917	31/03/1917
War Diary	Cul-de-Sac Estaires	06/04/1917	09/04/1917
War Diary	A.23.C.4 Steenwerck	13/04/1917	30/05/1917
War Diary	In The Field	02/06/1917	29/03/1918
Heading	25th Divisional Ammunition Column April 1918		
War Diary		02/04/1918	30/04/1918
War Diary	In The Field	01/05/1918	31/03/1919

WO/95/2234

14 Divisional Ammunition Column.

25TH DIVISION
DIVL ARTILLERY

25TH DIVL AMMN COLUMN
SEP 1915 - MAR 1919

25TH DIVISION
DIVL ARTILLERY

121/7594

35th Division

25th Brit: A.C.

Vol I

Sept & Oct 15

Nov '19

WAR DIARY
25th Divisional Ammunition Column.
or INTELLIGENCE SUMMARY.

Army Form C. 21

(Erase heading not required.)

Instructions regarding War Diaries and Intelligence Summaries are contained in F. S. Regs. Part II. and the Staff Manual respectively. Title pages will be prepared in manuscript.

Place	Date 1915	Hour	Summary of Events and Information	Remarks and references to Appendices
ALDERSHOT	Sept 27th	1.5 am & 8.20 am	The D.A.C. entrained for Southampton in 8 trains - weather dull & cloudy	
Southampton	"	4 pm	embarked on 3 ships MOUNT TEMPLE, PANCRAS, & ARCHITECT for HAVRE	
HAVRE	28th	8 am & 11 am	DAC disembarked at HAVRE - men & horses remained at HAVRE no 3 for the day. Vehicles parked near Prison ships - Heavy rain after 11 am	
"	"	9.20 pm	D.A.C entrained in 5 trains - Rain - 1 heavy draught horse died of colic	
en route	29th	8.20 am & 8.20 pm	HAZEBROUCK + marched to ST JANS CAPPEL	Reference maps
HAZEBROUCK	"	8.20 pm	RAC detrained at or near HAZEBROUCK weather fine	HAZEBROUCK
HAZEBROUCK	30th	7 am		BELGIUM
ST JANS CAPPEL	30th Oct 1st	3 am 5.30 pm	DAC arrived at ST JANS CAPPEL marched into billets. weather fine	IOCTOBER
"	"	-	filling up with ammunition - 1 mule died in No 2 Section - weather fine, all in the morning and evening	
"	2nd	"	D.A.C. Completed with ammunition - Fine day, calm, frosty morning.	
"	3rd	"	Fine day, calm, frosty morning. Heat quarters moved to NIEPPE on the BAILLEUL - NIEPPE road. East of the final E in LA CRECHE about 1½ miles WNW of the river cross roads	
"	4th	"	NIEPPE on the BAILLEUL - NIEPPE road. - Depot formed for issuing ammunition to Brigade Ammunition Columns from Divisional Sub-Park. - DAC remained at ST JANS CAPPEL motor convoy of Captain C.A.R. SCOTT. Guns shots heard at hed quarters - Issued 600 Shrapnel 120 H.E. to 112 Brigade R.F.A.	
			and 50. H.E. - 4.5 Hour to 113 Bde R.F.A. Weather Showery toward NE light. Horse died in No 1 Section of pneumonia.	
St Jans Cappel & point A.X	5th	"	Weather wet - 3 A.C. 05 + 15 mm Joined Head quarters from Sections	
"	6th	"	weather fine moving ammunition	
"	7th	"	do do do	

WAR DIARY
or
INTELLIGENCE SUMMARY.

(Erase heading not required.)

Army Form C. 2118

Instructions regarding War Diaries and Intelligence Summaries are contained in F. S. Regs., Part II. and the Staff Manual respectively. Title pages will be prepared in manuscript.

Place	Date	Hour	Summary of Events and Information	Remarks and references to Appendices
3 Section at ST JANS	1915 OCT 8th		Weather dull, slight East wind - ?? evening ?? ammunition	
CAPPEL Head quarters	9th		Weather dull & misty, slight East wind, issued ?? ammunition	
2¾ miles NNW of NIEPPE	10th		Weather fine. East wind & light. Three died of Pneumonia in No.1 Section	
on BAILLEUL - NIEPPE Road	11th		Weather fine in the morning, overcast in the evening, wind veered N.S.E, went to Cl JOHNS CAPPEL to enquire into the circumstances under which shots were fired by sentries, found that ?? did not justify their firing	
Reference	12		Wind veered S.W. Fine all day, atmosphere very clear in the evening	
?? ?? HAZEBROUCK	13		Wind veered S.W, gentle, rain.	
BELGIUM	14		Fine day	
??	15		Misty, calm - mule shot very ?? excellent	
	16		do	
	17		Commenced digging wells for water supply	
	18		Mostly calm. East wind	
	19		Calm. N.E fine but rather cloudy. commenced moving gravels from the ?? to ?? but ??	
	20		Cold. N.E wind slight fine	
	21		Cold. N.E wind slight, dull but dry, fine midday, ??, warmer in the afternoon, rain in the evening	
	22		Cold. S.E wind light but misty, warmer in the afternoon	
	23		Fine day, S.W wind gentle, warmer	
	24		Fine day	
	25		Misty S.E wind, morning and fine towards evening. Rain ?? ?? ?? heard from S.S.E ??	

WAR DIARY
or
INTELLIGENCE SUMMARY.
(Erase heading not required.)

Army Form C. 2118

Place	Date	Hour	Summary of Events and Information	Remarks and references to Appendices
As before	26		Fine day, wind East, dropping in the evening, rain in the evening	
	27		S.W. wind, light, showery, wind increased towards the evening, more rain	
	28		S.W. wind, fresh breeze, rain	
	29		S.W. wind, light, fine	
	30		S.W. wind, gentle, fine	
	31		S.E. wind, moderate, fine in the morning, occasional showers about 11 am, fine in the evening	

There has been nothing of military interest to report during this month — for the greater part of the month, the Head quarters with C.O. & Adjutant have been billeted about 1½ miles from NIEPPE on the BAILLEUL – NIEPPE Road, while No. 3 Section have been at ST JANS CAPPEL about 2 miles NNW of BAILLEUL. The ammunition supply has been from the 25th Divisional Sub Park & the Head quarters of the 25th DAC & from thence to the Brigade Ammunition Columns. The 3 Sections have been kept filled up with ammunition representing, has been issued from the Sections. They have been employed making lorries, repairing for the units generally — casualties to officers: none for the month, nil. There have been 24 Casualties with the month – 6 died, 2 discharged, rest of accident & 16 transferred to Motor Veterinary Section. The recruiting during October was generally fair, but during the last month we got but few men up to the usual standard, Forward will be Superior + that were have been very unlikely and many not up to the usual standard. Forward will be Superior + that section. 2nd Lt. Walsh was attached Temporary for duty, into the RE 2nd Division in 28th Section.

O M Black
Major
Comg 25th BAC

25th Sept.
Vol: 2

121/7693

25th Burann

Nov 15

Army Form C. 2118

WAR DIARY
or
INTELLIGENCE SUMMARY.
(Erase heading not required.)

25 Divisional Ammunition Column

Place	Date	Hour	Summary of Events and Information	Remarks and references to Appendices
Headquarters BNW 2½ miles of NIEPPE	1915 Nov 1		Wind ENE and inclined to fresh, rained all day, Clear frosty bright night	
BAILLEUL-NIEPPE Road near Mr Border of Wye road mill	2		Wind NE carried all day, weather improved towards evening, wind changed to NW, fresh breeze. 2 gunners joined from No 2 General base depot were posted to the 2 Section. N.W. wind increased in the morning, showery with fine intervals, calm in the evening, fine night	
STEENWERCK	3			
NEUVE EGLISE Road	4		frosty morning, cleared about 12 noon, calm, received new instructions as to Reserve of Ammunition to be maintained by Brigades of Infantry — Total Reserve for each Brigade 9000 1 rds — D.A.C. 3000 in Reserve Sub-Park 3000 ell 1 Reserve 2nd class Ammunition stopped (except 303 Rifle Ammunition, 2 Lighters Grenades the md of instructional purposes)	
The 3 Sections of DAC on the MONT NOIR — METEREN Road between K. Junction between above road & NAK 170 & FONTAINE HOUCK & LA MANCHE near ST JANS CAPPEL about 2 miles NNW of BAILLEUL Reference Map HAZEBROUCK 5-A	5		N.E. wind, bright, rain in the morning, frost in the afternoon colder, atmosphere clear, 8-10pm Shrapnel returned to Sub Park today, as they would not fit the breech could not be check. It was not known informed of the cause, but I suspect it must be due to want cartridges not having been bought to gauge before being refilled.	
	6		slight N.E. wind, hazy, colder. Sgt. Farrier A. Gray was transferred to the Base on account of being on the A.R. of Indian Corps.	
	7 am		N.E. wind, hazy, cold.	
	8 am		S.W. & W. wind, bright, warm. Had orders from all available mules to be exchanged for same number of picked out 210 mules. 195 heel & 75 wheel horses at HAZEBROUCK as the 10th A. used many mules & horses. Men are tired, handed over at HAZEBROUCK by the difficulty of keeping them shod up without Field Forge, while were lame owing to their difficulty, and also owing to the muddy standings, Boys also unattended to and had are greatly needed, but this a long job owing to the difficulty of getting timber or standings and being made, Enable for foundation	
BELGIUM				

WAR DIARY
or
INTELLIGENCE SUMMARY.

(Erase heading not required.)

Army Form C. 2118

Instructions regarding War Diaries and Intelligence Summaries are contained in F. S. Regs., Part II. and the Staff Manual respectively. Title pages will be prepared in manuscript.

Place	Date	Hour	Summary of Events and Information	Remarks and references to Appendices
As before	9th		S.W. wind, rain in the afternoon, wind strong lead in the evening. Doubtful information in October that Capt Elliott on the 17th instant took over command of 18/113 Brigade R.F.A. & Capt Hislops from the 113 Brigade B.A.C. took over command of No 1 Section B.A.C. in exchange.	
	10th		W. wind, moderate to light, showery to fine. The 18th cartridges returned on 6th apparently been extracted because the drawing bands were burnt. This might have been adopted by the Battery artificers. R.F.A. one gunner of No. 3 Section ex Field from Hospital at the base. S Williams & W.F.W Forward S.P.	R.F.A.
	11th		went west, light, fine in the morning, rained in the afternoon – 2 Leeds [?] & Ilchester, 2 [?] are posted to the Divisional Ammunition Column from Reserve Brigade of Ilchester, 2 [?] respectively. W.E. Emerson & A.C. Johnson reported to the 113th & 110th Battery R.F.A respectively. 1 Riding horse & 2 L.D. Horses were received were posted R.N.1 Section	
	12th		S.W. wind, strong, rained all day – The horses received by the Sections in exchange for the mules from the Indian Corps were of rather a lighter & smaller stamp, but quite satisfactory. The Section No.1 Section who received the same number of horses as the mules handed over except No 2 Section who received 8 heavy draught horses in exchange for 16 mules, each party retained their harness, except in the case of the H. 8 horses.	
	13th		N.W. wind, strong in the morning with rain, weather improved towards evening, fine clear night	
	14th		N.W. wind alight, colder, frost in the morning - 2 [?] Joined the B.A.C. this morning & was posted to the 2 Section	

Army Form C. 2118.

WAR DIARY
or
INTELLIGENCE SUMMARY
(Erase heading not required.)

Instructions regarding War Diaries and Intelligence Summaries are contained in F. S. Regs., Part II. and the Staff Manual respectively. Title pages will be prepared in manuscript.

Place	Date	Hour	Summary of Events and Information	Remarks and references to Appendices
As Before	15th		N.W. wind, cold & frosty morning, thawing, calm & fine.	
"	16		Frost gone, light cold, some rain in the afternoon, otherwise fine.	
	17		N.N.W. wind light with showers of rain, which up to 3 p.m. then fine, cold.	
	18		Hard frost last night, wind veered round to S.W., rained in the morning about 12 & then wind went round to the East again - clearing South and 5 gunners arrived from the base this afternoon per R.A.C.	
	19th		Frost last night - East wind cold, wind light.	
	20		Cold day, East wind light, Frost	
	21		Cold day, East wind light, Frost	
	22		Cold day - East wind light. Frost all day. Received orders today to send 2 officers + 70 men to-day trenches in the D.H.O line - 13 gunners + 1 observer, South-joined the B.E.F. from the base, Havre, without notice, this evening.	
	23rd		Cold in the morning, misty, East wind very light, Frosty in the morning, wind & rain in the evening - Four officers joined this column today from HAVRE - 2nd Lts W.H.H.PREECE,	

WAR DIARY
or
INTELLIGENCE SUMMARY.

(Erase heading not required.)

Army Form C. 2118

Place	Date	Hour	Summary of Events and Information	Remarks and references to Appendices
In billets	Nov 23rd		S.A. LANGE, E.F.H HARRISON, S.W. HARRIS and were posted, the first two to No 3 Section, and the last to No 1 Section. Lt H.H. RIDDICK to 3 Section & 2 Lt FORREST 2 Section were posted to 111th Brigade RFA – 2 Lt SWINFORD to 2 Section and 2 Lt S. WILLIAMS to 1 Section & 112th Bde RFA. 7 other Ranks reported their arrival at D.A.C. Head quarters 4 gunners, 1 Sergt, 2 Corporals & 2 Bombardiers, were to 1113th Bde RFA and are Bombardier to 110th Bde RFA & 1 to S.S.T. 111 Brigade. 2 officers also reported arrival 2nd Lt R.C.L. Williams & F.A.O. Murray both to 113th Bde RFA	
	24		N.W. wind, light, warmer – This evening about 8pm / M – S. Smithies & others passed from Mrs Bruce HAVRE. One cheery smile from the 40 mtn brigade.	
	25		N. W. wind, light, fine, until the afternoon, then a little rain.	
	26th		N.W. wind in the morning, veering round to E – showers of sleet until about 2 whn fine, cold. 3 showers. Smiths & 5 others arrived today from the line.	
	27		Cold, frosty & fine day. E. wind light. The horses are now in their brick standings, the men in huts, the barn is used as a dining mess-room – canteen. They have tables, forms, someplates, mugs, re. gramophone and they are fully comfortable. the men who arrived yesterday were all posted to this section.	
	28th		Very cold all day. S.E. wind most of the day, light – 2nd Lt Beaver Jones & was posted to No 2 section	
	29h		S.E. wind, strong, increasing in strength in the evening. Snowed at intervals during the day. horses much excited 2 with Harris No 1 Section transferred to 110th Bde R.F.A. One horse destroyed at Head quarters on account of Tetanus.	

Army Form C. 2118

WAR DIARY
or
INTELLIGENCE SUMMARY.
(Erase heading not required.)

Place	Date	Hour	Summary of Events and Information	Remarks and references to Appendices
Havre	Nov 23rd		S.A. LANGE, E.F.H. HARRISON, S.W. HARRIS and were posted the first two to No 3 Section, the 3rd to No 2 Section and the last to No 1 Section. 2nd Lt FORREST 2nd Section was posted to 111th Brigade RFA. 2 2nd Lt SWINFORD to 2 Section and 2nd Lt S. WILLIAMS to 1 Section to 112 Bde RFA. 7 Other Ranks reported their arrival at DAC Head Quarters of whom 1 Sergt, 2 Corporals & 2 Bombardiers went on to 113th Bde RFA and one Bombardier to 110th Bde RFA and S.S. to 111th Brigade. on to 113th Bde RFA and J.A.O. Murray both to 113th Bde RFA. 2 officers also reported arrival 2nd Lt R.C.L. Williams & J.A.O. Murray both to 113th Bde RFA.	
	24		N.W. wind, light, warmer. This evening about 6pm /Bdr. S. Smithe & 9 drivers joined from the Base - HAVRE. Our cheery smith from the 40th Brigade.	
	25		N.W. wind, light, fine mostly the afternoon, thin & little rain.	
	26th		N.W. wind in the morning, veering round to E - showers of sleet and hail about 2 when fire, cold.	
	27		3 cheery Smiths & 5 drivers arrived today from the Base. Cold, Frosty & fine day. E wind light. The huts are now in their trick standings, the men in huts, the Barn is used as a dining room & Canteen. They have hitherto formed ample place rugs no gramophone and they are pretty comfortable. The men who arrived yesterday were all posted to this section.	
	28th		Very cold all day. S.E. wind most of the day, light - 2nd Lt Stewart joined & was posted to No 2 Section	
	29h		S.E. wind strong, increasing in strength in the evening. Damned at intervals during the day. Horse parade exercise 2nd Lt Stewart No 1 Section transferred to 110 Bde RFA. One horse destroyed at Head Quarters on account of Tetanus.	

WAR DIARY
or
INTELLIGENCE SUMMARY
(Erase heading not required.)

Army Form C. 2118

Place	Date	Hour	Summary of Events and Information	Remarks and references to Appendices
As before	30th		S.W. wind, moderate, fine weather.	
			The following casualties have occurred during the month.	
			Officers joined — Officers left. — other ranks joined — other ranks left. — animals joined — animals left.	
			41 — 15 Transport 194 Lithorses 210 mules & Indian Coys.	
			2nd Lt Tomaron to 110th Bde 12/11/15 — 8 wounded Sick — 8 N.I. — 1 horse died	
			Lieut Ruddick to 111th Bde 23/11/15 — 26 horses — 1 mule & destroyed	
			2nd Lieut Emerson to 113th Bde 12/11/15 — 3 horses & destroyed	
			2nd " Shorthouse to 112th Bde 23/11/15 — 10 mules & invalided	
			" Forrest to 110th Bde — 8 horses & invalided sick	
			" Sumford " 112th Bde do	
			2nd Lt Harris 110th Bde 29/11/15	
			Snowfield 10.11.15	
			Harris 23.11.15	
			Hannon "	
			Longe "	
			Reese "	
			Dewar 29.11.15	
			Nothing of military interest to report as far as this Column is concerned during the month.	
			A.M. Block	
			Lt Col	
			Comdg 23rd Bde R.F.A.	

25th S.A.C.
Vol. 3

7294
/21

Army Form C. 2118.

WAR DIARY
or
INTELLIGENCE SUMMARY.
(Erase heading not required.)

25th J.F.C.

Place	Date 1915	Hour	Summary of Events and Information	Remarks and references to Appendices
Head quarters a. BAILLEUL	Decr 1		S.W. wind, fine until the afternoon, then wind increased & a little rain, one Heavy draught horse in No 2 Section shot today, suffering from Pneumonia Lineseuth	
ARMENTIERES	2nd		Went N.W. finer. mild.	
Rue du Bois de la Meute	3rd		East wind in the morning, much frain, changing to S.W. with more wind & rain. Heavy frost at night. Night	
FIEUVE EGLISE	4th		S.W. wind & rain all day.	
Section of M.D.A.C. at	5th		Calm & fine until evening - wind what there was from S.W.	
	6th		S.W. wind strong, fine until midday. then rain all the afternoon & night	
ST JANS CAPPEL	7th		S.W. wind moderate, rained in the afternoon.	
	8th		S.W. wind, light, fine all day, fine night	
Sect STA HAZEBROUCK	9th		S.E wind in the morning. Wind changed to S.W wind at night wind rain	
BELGIUM	10		S.W. wind strong, rain in the morning & fine the rest of the day.	
	11		N.W. wind strong rain, all ditches full, after rain by getting flooded. Today the New guardians moved to ST JANS CAPPEL, Mr Clifford relieved Mr Sampson at supply my place their being taken by Capt Fitzgerald from R.O. No 2 Section, Capt Elliot from B/NS taking over command of the 2 Section	
	12		N.W. wind moderate & light, showers at intervals, weather improving. Colder. 1 Chap or No 23 L. & win. arrived today Strength established.	

2353 Wt. W2544/1454 700,000 5/15 D. D. & L. A.D.S.S./Forms/C. 2118.

Army Form C. 2118.

WAR DIARY
or
INTELLIGENCE SUMMARY. of 25th F.A.C

(Erase heading not required.)

Instructions regarding War Diaries and Intelligence Summaries are contained in F. S. Regs., Part II. and the Staff Manual respectively. Title pages will be prepared in manuscript.

Place	Date	Hour	Summary of Events and Information	Remarks and references to Appendices
Hazebrouck	Dec 1915 13th		N.W. wind, fine, cold. 1 horse destroyed, broken leg.	
to 9 Section at	14		N.W. wind, slight frost at night - cold all day	
St JANS CAPPEL	15		S.W. wind, fine. slight	
and detachment at period	16		S.W. wind gentle, weather misty	
	17		Calm, rained most of the day, misty	
at BAILLEUL	18		Misty, East wind very gentle, clearer in the afternoon.	
ARMENTIERES and near to	19		East wind, light, fine day, the smell of gas was noticed here this morning, although about 10 miles from the trenches.	
Junction with NEUVE EGLISE	20		Wind N.W. light, cloudy, misty in the evening	
Sheet 5A	21		Wind N.W. very gentle, rain	
HAZEBROUCK BELGIUM 1/100000	22		N.W. & wind, rain.	
	23		W & S.W. wind, rain	
	24		S.W. wind strong, fine day, sunshine	
	25		N.W. wind rained a great part of the day	
	26		N.W. wind fine day sunshine nearly all day	
	27		S.W. wind cold rain	
	28		S.W. wind sunshine	
	29		wind N.W. fine day	
	30		wind N.W. cloudy, stormy, misty	

Army Form C. 2118.

WAR DIARY
or
INTELLIGENCE SUMMARY. 25th D.A.C.

(Erase heading not required.)

Place	Date	Hour	Summary of Events and Information	Remarks and references to Appendices
As before	Dec 31st		S.E wind light, rain. No incident of any military interest occurred during the month. The Ammunition Column has not been used for the supply of ammunition. The work during the month has been, making truck standings, huckerout roads etc. As the supply of bricks has been plentiful, the horse standings are nearing completion, but a great deal still remains to be done in making huckerout roads. The casualties during the month have been as follows. Officers:- Capt Elliott from R/113 Bde RFA to Command Bo 2 Section Capt Fitzgerald from Comdg Bo 2 Section to Ammunition Supply Depot. 88 N.C.O men joined from the base. 1 ,, ,, from 111 H.B.A. Men transfd to {1 to 111th Brigade, 1 to 112th Brigade, 4 to 113th Brigade} 12 joined. 7 men evacuated to Base, sick. 1 ,, sent to Base, under age. Horses 23 Light draught joined in 12 Decr. 1 charger. Horses 3 - died 4 - destroyed 14 - evacuated A.M.Block Bt Col Comdg 25th D.A.C.	

25th Divisional Artillery

25th DIVISIONAL AMMUNITION COLUMN

JANUARY   1916

Army Form C. 2118.

WAR DIARY
or
INTELLIGENCE SUMMARY.   25th Divisional Ammunition Column.

(Erase heading not required.)

Instructions regarding War Diaries and Intelligence
Summaries are contained in F. S. Regs., Part II.
and the Staff Manual respectively. Title pages
will be prepared in manuscript.

Place	Date, 1916	Hour	Summary of Events and Information	Remarks and references to Appendices
Head Quarters at SCHAEKKEN cross roads	JAN 1		S.W. wind, showery gale in the evening, rainy to fine in the afternoon & evening; wind decreasing in the night	
	2nd		S.W. wind, gale to moderate rain after 11 a.m., rain increased towards evening & then stopped	
	3		Fine morning. W. wind	
1 Kilometre W/ of ST. JANS CAPPEL – 3 Section	4th		Dull S.W. wind, rain in the afternoon	
	5		Fine morning, dull afternoon	
in METEREN	6		S.W. wind, rainy a little during day, dull	
– MONT-NOIRS and road from 2 ft. chow to	7		S.W. wind, rain in afternoon, fine towards evening, wind veering NNW.	
farm de N.W. of Wt. Junction of	8		N. wind, fine, colder	
Wat road with	9		West wind, fine	
road to MONT DES CATS	10		West wind, fine	
3 Section S.W. of SCHAEXKEN Cross roads.	11		West wind, fine, a little rain in the afternoon	
	12		do do	
No 1 Section at a farm 200 x	13.		N.W. wind, showery, fine in the afternoon	
S.W. of same Corr road.	14		N.W. wind - fine	
No 3 Section at LA MANCHE farm about 600 x N.E. of same Corr roads.	15		N.W. wind - fine but dull – Today 1 officer, 120 men, 224 horses left to take over A.S.C. duties at STEENTJE while the horses of the 25th Divl Train are being "mallieined", 2nd Lt LANGE in command. 2nd Lt H. BURKE JACKLIN joined. were posted to No 2 Section	
Reference Sheet S.A HAZEBROUCK	16		Fine day S.W. wind	

BELGIUM 1
100 000

Army Form C. 2118.

WAR DIARY
or
INTELLIGENCE SUMMARY. 25th DAC

(Erase heading not required.)

Instructions regarding War Diaries and Intelligence Summaries are contained in F. S. Regs., Part II. and the Staff Manual respectively. Title pages will be prepared in manuscript.

Place	Date 1916 January	Hour	Summary of Events and Information	Remarks and references to Appendices
Hondeghem	17		S.W. wind dull in the morning, rain afternoon & evening.	
Depot of a point about 100° East of junction of BAILLEUL - NIEPPE & STEENWERCK - NEUVE EGLISE roads.			a detachment consisting of 2 Officers 2nd Lts DEWAR & HARRISON – 139 other ranks 156 horses & 38 wagons a proportionate number from each of the 3 Sections left H'te overnight at the H.Q of L.S CRÈCHE, near STEENWERCK - RÉLÉNE Sheet 5A, HAZEBROUCK, BELGIUM trees — for the purpose of transporting Road material from the siding at STEENWERCK station.	
	18th		S.W. wind very light, damp & raining	
	19		S.W. wind light, fine until the evening. Haze during the night had a little rain	
	20		wind veered N.W., fine morning & afternoon, some rain at intervals – Received orders that the D.A.C. would move on 25th to BORRE near HAZEBROUCK.	
	21		S.W. wind dull some rain – orders for move of D.A.C. cancelled. 2/Lt LANGE transferred to 112 Bde R.F.A.	
	22		S.W. wind some showers at intervals. detachment returned from STEENTJE.	
	23		⎫	
	24		Fine little or no wind, what there was from the West. N.W. & S.W.	
	25		⎭	
	26		Fine calm, evening wind what there was.	
	27th		Dull, rain in the afternoon, S.W. & W. wind very light	
	28		Dull – S.W. very light, misty & rainy. fine afternoon	
	29h		Dull but fine, little or no wind, what there was went round to East in the evening	
	30		Dull misty damp – East wind very light	

WAR DIARY
or
INTELLIGENCE SUMMARY. 25th Divisional Ammunition Column.

Army Form C. 2118.

Place	Date 1916	Hour	Summary of Events and Information	Remarks and references to Appendices
Outpost	Jan 31		Nothing during the month worthy of note except faults. The following casualties have occurred amongst officers & other ranks. TRANSFERRED 2nd Lieut W. Burke joined 1st D.A.C. R.F.A. Large number transferred to 110, 111, 112, 113 Bde RFA 10-1-16 2nd Lieut H. Burke Jacklin 25th Div L Train 7-1-16 123 H.B. Right 17-1-16	
			61 Other ranks transferred 7-1-16	
			28 " " " joined 8-1-16	
			1 " " " " 12-1-16	
			3 " " " " 14-1-16	
			15 " " " " 17-1-16	
			15 " " " " 22-1-16	
			50 " " " " died	
			8 " " " " 30-1-16	
			1 " " sick & 2 others died, all evacuated to hospital during month.	
			HORSES	
			34 Horses joined	
				3 Horses died, ruptured stomach, pneumonia
				2 Horses shot, result from accident
				2 mules shot - accident & tetanus
				13 Horses mules evacuated {sick, 10 2 D, 1 H D, 1 mule}
			The work carried on during the month consisted mainly in supplying lorries & fatigues for RE & ASC, 62 officers retired 40 mm engaged in ammunition supply in the ammunition depot. No military incident reported.	

A M Blocksiche
Commanding
25th Div: Amm: Col: R.F.A.

25th DIVISIONAL ARTILLERY

25th DIVISIONAL AMMUNITION COLUMN

FEBRUARY 1916

Army Form C. 2118.

WAR DIARY
or
INTELLIGENCE SUMMARY. 25th S.A.C.
(Erase heading not required.)

Instructions regarding War Diaries and Intelligence Summaries are contained in F. S. Regs., Part II. and the Staff Manual respectively. Title pages will be prepared in manuscript.

Place	Date 1916	Hour	Summary of Events and Information	Remarks and references to Appendices
Hazebrouck + Station	1st February		NE wind very light cold + fine. Nothing to report.	
on work	2nd to 8th		Nothing to report.	
	9th		2nd Lieut IRONSIDE arrived was posted to No 2 Section	
METEREN	10th		Fine + cold N wind light	
— MONT NOIR	11th		Wind Sly E, rain, cold.	
between	12–14		Nothing to report, wind generally from S.W+W. unsettled weather.	
LA MANCHE on the North + and junction	15th		Strong N.W wind cold, dropped in the evening.	
	16		Pleas. hard frost S.W during night 15–16 + during the morning; rain up to 11am, afterwards fine and unsettled.	
N of H.Q.	17		Fine wind N.W. not light	
FONTAINE HOUCK	18		Rain - calm. Lt Hughes joined	
H.-Croix	19		Wind N.W + calm	
Detachment employed on	20		Wind East - aeroplanes active. Colder at night	
army road	21		Fine, cold, S.E wind very light	
	22–25		Easterly, south easterly winds, cold mornings 2 alts Cavanagh and Dixon joined on 25th posted to No 1 + 2 Sections respectively	
LA CRÈCHE 2½ miles SE	26		Gale in the morning, became at midday, rain in the afternoon, S. E wind.	
	27		S. W wind rain	
	28		Fine day - N.W wind slight.	
BAILLEUL	29		Showery — were sent to attempt what stopped work totally cold but and import, too everywhere not working	

Army Form C. 2118.

WAR DIARY
or
INTELLIGENCE SUMMARY. 25th Bde

(Erase heading not required.)

Place	Date	Hour	Summary of Events and Information	Remarks and references to Appendices
	29th Feb		Officers joined { 2nd Lt Ironside K.L., 2nd Lt Pearce R.F.A. 2nd Lt A.W. Hughes Jnr attd R.F.A. 2nd Lt E.H. Dixon Sr Res R.F.A. 2nd Lt A.J. Cunningham	Officers left 2nd Lt F.M. Walsh to 113 How Bat Capt C.A.R. Scott to 38 Bde R.F.A. 2nd Lt W.F. Menzies to 28 Tr Morter
			Other ranks joined 74. Transferred to Brigade R.F.A. B Sec 120 / 1 / in the Battery from Ammunition Column	
			Remounts received 15 mules evacuated 5 died 1 (Ammn Col)	
			At end of Rubicon no ponies to mount	
				A.W.R.Hockin? Br Gen Comdg 25th Bde

25th DIVISIONAL ARTILLERY

25th DIVISIONAL AMMUNITION COLUMN

MARCH 1916

WAR DIARY
or
INTELLIGENCE SUMMARY.

Army Form C. 2118.

25th Divisional Ammunition Column

Place	Date	Hour	Summary of Events and Information	Remarks and references to Appendices
Headquarters & Nos 2 & 3 Sections in the ...	1st March		Fine day – digging party, 1 Officer & 50 men returned from NIEPPE. Bomb dropped by aeroplane near to 2 Section.	
	2nd		Fine morning, wet afternoon	
METEREN	3rd		Dull hot first in the morning, about 3 pm it began to hail violent slowly with N.E. wind which later until midday of the 4th worked thru clouds up, sun did not W.	
MONT NOIR road N & S of SCHAERKEN	4th			
Kelmode W.N.W. of JAN'S CAPPEL	5th		Saw absence of wheels stenuous fine. N.E. wind 4/4. Establishment of wagons received in respect of reduction of S.A.A. carried in the reduction on the number of Batteries in the Howitzer Brigade from 4 to 3.	
No 1 Section at LA CRECHE Sect 5A			Old Establishment E.1098. New Establishment	
			18 pr ammn. 57 wagons 18 pr – 58 wagons	
			4.5" – 12 4.5" – 9	
			S.A.A. 26 (includes 1 extra wagon pr S.A.A. – 21	
			Pioneer Battalion) 86	
			95 H.Q. 3	
			3 89	
			98	
HAZEBROUCK BELGIUM 100 000	6—		7 L.D. horses from No 2 Section 1/VII Brigade R.F.A. No 1 Section returned today. N.E wind light. Snow shown in the morning, bright afterwards	
			from LA CRECHE.	
	7—		Snowed the whole day. (1) 2/Lt DENNIS & ALSTON & Temporary 2/Lt FRASER, ROSE & WISE joined the DAC. Lts 2 & Lts HARRISON, BURGE, TACKLIN, IRONSIDE & DEAN left. (2) S.R. from Pizza Hill (3) from 112th Bde RFA (4) 113th Bde R/FA (5) to 28th Trench mortar Battery (6) to 113th Bde. RFA (7) R.T.M 2 Bde RFA.	
			(1) from RMA returned. (2) (3) (4)	

Army Form C. 2118.

WAR DIARY
or
INTELLIGENCE SUMMARY. 25th D.A.C

(Erase heading not required.)

Instructions regarding War Diaries and Intelligence Summaries are contained in F.S. Regs., Part II. and the Staff Manual respectively. Title pages will be prepared in manuscript.

Place	Date	Hour	Summary of Events and Information	Remarks and references to Appendices
Head quarters & 3 Section of Bn	8		Fine day, calm, clear.	
METEREN	9		Sun.	
MONT NOIR and N+S of SCHAEXKEN	10		The D.A.C left SCHAEXKEN at 8 am & marched via BAILLEUL - OUTERSTEEN - VIEUX BERQUIN - MERVILLE & HAVERSKERQUE & went into billets near that place. No men in muddy fields, horses along the roadside. Moved on from the motortrans. but action inverted about 5pm.	
SCHAEXKEN	11		Very wet morning, though HAVERSKERQUE - SAINS LES PERNES. D.A. marched to SAINS LES PERNES via ST VENANT - LILLERS - PERNES - SAINS LES PERNES. 1 Kilometre weather cold wind & gradually during the day.	
1 Kilometre WNW of ST JANS CAPPEL			Trops shed SM HAZEBROUCK - BELGIUM 100000 & Shed SM 11 - LENS - FRANCE 100000	
			Left at 9.15 - Next quarters to Br 3 Section, followed by Br 1 Section. & Br 2 Section at ½ hour intervals arrived about 3.30pm & 4.30 pm. Billeted at SAINS LES PERNES. Horses all in one field - horses as usual.	
H.Q. & 3 Sections at SAINS LES PERNES. 11 - LENS - FRANCE 100000	12		SAINS LES PERNES, each section a separate unit. Weather cold, calm, raw. Cold morning, fine afternoon inverted.	
	13		Fine day, cold morning	
	14		Fine day. 2nd Lt Hughes transferred to 112th R.F.A. 2nd Lt Berens, 2nd Lt Cunningham & M"Bede	
	15		Fine day. 2nd Lt Alston & Fraser to 112th R.F.A. Lieut. JAMIESON posted 2nd Lt Evans to 112" Bde, 2 Lt ALSTON & FRASER to 113" Bde RFA - Lieut JAMIESON posted.	
	16		R.A.C from 111 to B.R.F.A Fine in the morning & little rain afternoon	
	17		Marched at 11 am via TANGRY - VALHUON - ST POL & The following billets - H.Q. & M/Section to MAISNIL ST-POL - No 2 Section to 03 Coeurs to 3 Section & TACHINCOURT - Section at ½ hour intervals. Fine day.	
	18		Halted. Fine day.	

WAR DIARY or INTELLIGENCE SUMMARY. 25th D.A.C.

Army Form C. 2118.

Place	Date	Hour	Summary of Events and Information	Remarks and references to Appendices
Headquarters	19th & 20th		Fine days.	
No 1 Section at	20 – 23rd		Some rain, colder. Received orders that in future the proportion of 18 pr Shrapnel + H.E. was to be 70% + 30% respectively. C.R.A. XVII Corps inspected lines of Column.	
MAISNIL ST POL	24th		Received 1872 rounds of A. for 18 pr. 25th Divn. also received HE sent 25th Divn. also aux. parks	
No 2 Section at OCOCHE			2014 boxes MILLS grenades returned to No 22nd ords workshops of Ba.R.W. & 25 Divn H.Q.	
			Sent for movements of Infantry Brigades	
No 3 Section at	25th		Heavy snowfall.	
	26th		Very cold some snow.	
TACHINCOURT	26th		Cold strong. Church Parade service held in Lecture 77th F.O. Amb. – A.P.M. called with reference to Spinde heavy shell in boarbanck in MAISNIL – acts sawbones – put up notices forbidding such practices.	
Reference Map SHEET 11 LENS FRANCE 1/100,000	27th		Inspected by Major General former M.A. at 2-30 p.m. – very cold – much rain – the Sanitary Officer expressed himself as satisfied with the condition of the horse and men + except those more than animals in N° 1 Section – at 8 p.m. – received from 25th Div Am Park 2,500 Grenades Hand N° 1 + 1520 Grenades Hand N° 2 – 20 Detonators Delivered	
	28th		A Board assembled to check all ammunition with L. Mr Coleman – Papers received from O.C. N° 2 Section of the death of driver of N°. 74,538 A.T.S. Evans – Fine day.	
	29th		Board held for inquiring into Cause of death of N° Evans also of 9 boxes of ammun Shrapnel 18 pr. A	

Fine day. April of 3 pmLS signature A.B.S.S. Forms/C. 2118.

WAR DIARY

Army Form C. 2118.

INTELLIGENCE SUMMARY. 23rd D.A.C.

(Erase heading not required.)

Place	Date	Hour	Summary of Events and Information	Remarks and references to Appendices
MAISNIL ST POL	3/16 30th		Two Officers arrived from HAVRE & one footed to return but afterwards sent on to Brigades in accordance with instructions received later. Attended a funeral service for the late R. EVANS.	
	3/31		Transfers:- 2nd Lt. A.H. Smith, 2 shoeing smiths, 11 Gunners, 7 Drivers to 110 Brigade RFA	
	"		" W.R. Loader, 1 shoeing smith, 2 saddlers, 18 Gunners, 14 Drivers to 111 Bde RFA	
	"		" 2nd Lt. Jensen, 17 Gunners, 5 Drivers to 112 Brigade RFA	
	"		" 2nd Lt. H. Jennings, 11 Gunners, 4 Drivers to 113 Brigade RFA	
	"		" 1 Sergeant to overseas. Sent to reform Z.25 Trench Mortar Battery	
	"		Attached:- 1 Sub-Section of No 3 Section sent for duty to the 51st Divisional Artillery - viz 2nd Lt. Luce 43 other ranks + 9 Officers' Servants	
			Fine day. Sunshine. Calm. Cold in the evening. 3000 Glenares Mills No5 received from Art. Command Park 25th Divn	

Posted during month
12 Officers
88 O.R
Horses
9 came

Transferred
13 Officers
126 O.R
Horses
= 45

Struck off
1 Officer
28 O.R
1 O.R.

Horses remounted
28

Horses dead
1 died of colic
1 destroyed

Death
1 O.R.

A.M. Block
Br. Col.
Comy 23rd Bde RFA

25th DIVISIONAL ARTILLERY

25th DIVISIONAL AMMUNITION COLUMN

APRIL 1916

25. DAP
Vol. 7

Army Form C. 2118.

WAR DIARY
or
INTELLIGENCE SUMMARY. 25—D.A.C.

(Erase heading not required.)

Instructions regarding War Diaries and Intelligence Summaries are contained in F.S. Regs., Part II. and the Staff Manual respectively. Title pages will be prepared in manuscript.

Place	Date 1916	Hour	Summary of Events and Information	Remarks and references to Appendices
Headquarters	1 April		Fine day. Wind light	
No 1 Section	2nd		Fine day, warmer	
MAISNIL ST PAL	3rd		Fine – warm. 13. O.R. joined from base.	
No 2 Section	4th		Dull – colder. 13. O.R. transferred to Brigades.	
	5		Dull morning, fine afternoon	
at OCOCHE	6		Dull – cold. N.E. wind light	
No 3 Section	7		Dull – cold. N.E. wind light – Capt FITZGERALD. H.C. Transferred to 31st Divn. to command A/170 Bde. RFA	
No 3 Section	8		Fine day, cold wind. N.E. slight. 62 O.R. joined from Base – Capt Vincent from 112 Bde RFA to command	
	9 + 10th		No 3 Section notes offset from 7.4.16. 7 O.R. joined from base on the 10th	
TACHINCOURT	11		Fine days – S.W. wind light.	
1 Section	12		Rainy – S.W. Wind strong. Capt Walkern left today to go through a course at LARK HILL	
of No 3 Section			Rain all day. – S.W. wind strong.	
at BERLES	13		N. Westerly strong, generally fine. 19. O.R. arrived today from Base.	
	14		N.W wind moderate & light – showers at intervals, generally fine, cold	
Rly Shed No 11	15		N.W. wind light, fine, warmer	
FRANCE. LENS	16		Fine day, little or no wind	
FRANCE	17		rain part of the day S.W. wind	
100000	18		rain all day. S.W. wind	
	19		Rain – S.W. wind	
	20		N.W wind, fine.	
	21		S.W. wind, fine morning	

Army Form C. 2118.

Instructions regarding War Diaries and Intelligence Summaries are contained in F.S. Regs., Part II. and the Staff Manual respectively. Title pages will be prepared in manuscript.

WAR DIARY
or
INTELLIGENCE SUMMARY. 25th DHQ

(Erase heading not required.)

Place	Date	Hour	Summary of Events and Information	Remarks and references to Appendices
Headquarters + No 2 & 3 Section at VILLERS BRULIN	22 April		Rained all day. Head Quarters + Nos 2 & 3 Sections marched at 10 am to VILLERS BRULIN about 2 miles North of SAVY. No 1 Section remained at MAISNIL ST POL, arrived about 2 pm.	
No 2 & 3 Sections at VILLERS BRULIN No 1 Section at MAISNIL ST POL	23rd April		Fine day. N.W. wind. No 3 Section detached 1 Sergt + 19 men to take up duties at MAROEUIL under XVII Corps Heavy Artillery in connection with Ammunition Canteen, viz 1 Officer, 38 O.R., 52 Horses + 8 wagons for fatigues at ECROIVES Station, 6 horses + 18 S. Wagons for fatigues at A.C.Q., 4 prisoners for French station at ECROIVES - Supply personnel the Ammunition dump at A.C.Q., 4 prisoners for French station at ECROIVES + R.S.M. WHITEBREAD to Grenade store.	
	24th April		Fine day. S.W. wind light.	
	25 + 26		Fine days, warm. Received 156 trades instead of L.O. Horses transferred to Brigades	
	27th April		Fine warm day. No 2 Section marched to ECROIVES. Who employed there in connection with French Light Railway.	
	28th		Fine warm day, light breeze from the East. 33 men arrived from the base.	
	29th		Fine day, fresh breeze from the East. No 1 Section marched in from MAISNIL ST POL	
	30		Fine day, warm - breeze from the East. The remainder of No 3 Section moved to ECROIVES. No 2 Section + part of No 3 Section exclusive of detachment at ECROIVES STATION Ammunition Dump, Grenade store + MAROEUIL took over duties of the Light railway for outlying stores etc to the trenches.	

Army Form C. 2118.

WAR DIARY
or
INTELLIGENCE SUMMARY. 25th B.A.C.

(Erase heading not required.)

Place	Date	Hour	Summary of Events and Information	Remarks and references to Appendices
			During the month of April the following Casualties occurred.	
			Officers posted	
			2nd Lt WARD from 110th Bde on promotion	
			2nd Lt J. MILLER from B.S.M. 1st & 3 Section RAC	
			2nd Lt S. PAGE " " " " 1 Section DAC	
			Officers Evacuated	
			Captain H.C. FITZGERALD to A/170 Bde RFA	
			Other Ranks	
			147 from the Base	
			Horses & Mules	
			26	
			Other Ranks	
			29 to Brigades 25 Divnl Artillery	
			1 to 29th Battery RFA	
			1 to Base on Completion of service	
			Horses & Mules Evacuated	
			27 —	
			1 Horse destroyed gunshot gunshot	
			1 mule Rupture of intestines	

30/4/16

A.W.Black
Bt Lt Col
Cmg 25th BAC

25th DIVISIONAL ARTILLERY

25th DIVISIONAL AMMUNITION COLUMN

MAY 1916

D.A.G. C.81
3rd Echelon

I forward herewith War Diary of
25th D.A.C. in accordance with G.R.O 1598
d 30.5.16.

AM Block
3 6/16   Bde
Comg 25 DAC

DCC 25 JW
VOL 8

(Army Form C. 2118.)

WAR DIARY
or
INTELLIGENCE SUMMARY. 25 BAC
(Erase heading not required.)

Instructions regarding War Diaries and Intelligence Summaries are contained in F.S. Regs., Part II. and the Staff Manual respectively. Title pages will be prepared in manuscript.

Place	Date 19/6	Hour	Summary of Events and Information	Remarks and references to Appendices
Head quarters & No 1 Section at	1st May	—	Fine day, East wind light. 20 men on detachment at MAROEUIL joined this Section (No 3)	
	2nd	—	Fine day, with an thunder shower.	
VILLERS BRULIN	3rd	—	Fine. S.W. wind light. 1 corporal & 5 gunners to be driven away from Base. Corporal to No 1 Section, the remainder attached to No 3.	
No 2 & No 3	4th	—	Fine day. Casually one mule killed & mostly four others & one mule injured by the light railway, one man injured (67514 Driver G. WILLIAMS 2nd Section)	
Section (less a detachment of	5th	—	Dull but fine — 80 O.R. transferred to 6th Brigade AC	
I.O.-38 O.R. 58 horses at	6th	—	Fine day, colder at night	
ECROIVES STATION	7th	—	Showery all day, colder — S.W. wind moderate	
I.M.C.O.-22 gunners	8th	—	Showery. S.W. wind moderate. Head quarters moved today at 10 am to LE PENDU. B.RANSOM (64443) to 2 Sect — A mine crater dump near to LE PENDU — 1 mile Not ACQ	
5 horses at ACQ)	9th	—	was accidentally wounded by the explosion of a bomb whilst firing manure in an incinerator — All	
at ECROIVES	10	—	Showery. S.W. wind strong, cold. a horse shot in light railway on night of 9/10.	
	11	—	Fine.	
Refer map 1	12	—	Cold + dull, some rain early.	
LENS, FRANCE	13	—	Fine but dull	
10/5/16	14	—	Pleasant morn & flat day. S.W. wind	
	15	—	Dull, cold + damp. One horse killed on light railway	
	16	—	Dull mule killed on light railway	
	17	—	Fine day	
	18	—	Fine day	
	19	—	Fine day	
	20	—	Windy day. This was the last time that 2 + 3 Section worked the light railway as do. No 1 Section marched tonight from VILLERS BRULIN to MAISNIL ST POL a/a 8.30 pm	

2353   Wt. W2544/1454   700,000   5/15   D.D. & L.   A.D.S.S./Forms/C. 2118.

WAR DIARY or INTELLIGENCE SUMMARY

Army Form C. 2118.

Place	Date	Hour	Summary of Events and Information	Remarks and references to Appendices
No 1 Section MAISNIL	21st		Fine day. No 1 Section arrived at MAISNIL ST POL – draft of 8 O.R. arrived yesterday from Base.	
Nos 2 & 3 Sections at VILLERS BRULIN	22nd		Fine morning, afternoon some rain fell. 15 beams from No 2 & 3 Sections to work on light railway.	
	23rd		Nos 2 & 3 Sections left at 8.30 pm for VILLERS BRULIN.	
VILLERS BRULIN	24th		Fine morning. Battle practice afternoon & evening – 2 O.R. arrived from base.	
Headquarters & two troops at LE PENDU	25th		Fine day on the whole, movement from S.W.	
Reference map 1/100,000 LENS FRANCE	26th		The B.A.C. was reorganised today. – The B.A.C.s of 110", 111" & 112" Brigades became the nucleus of Section 1, 2 & 3 of A echelon. 113" & B A.C. is attached, the 12 Howitzer ammunition wagons to the lectional cars are divided between 1, 2 & 3 Sections. No 4 Section is formed from the remains of the old 1, 2 & 3 Section after 1, 2 & 3 Section of A echelon are complete with horses men, Draught Men horses & G.S. wagons being exchanged with time have. No 1 Section marched in from MAISNIL ST POL. No 1 Section Capt ELLIOT being up – Capt SHERD from 118 "Bde K.F." commands No 3 & Captain PARKINS from 111" B.A.C. commands No 2. Capt LYNCH commands No 4 – The surplus horses, men & 10 other G.S. wagon left by mid march for ABBEVILLE.	
	27		Process of Reorganisation continuing – Horse breeder wagons from LE PENDU to VILLERS BRULIN.	

Army Form C. 2118.

WAR DIARY
or
INTELLIGENCE SUMMARY. 25th DAC.

(Erase heading not required.)

Instructions regarding War Diaries and Intelligence Summaries are contained in F. S. Regs., Part II. and the Staff Manual respectively. Title pages will be prepared in manuscript.

Place	Date	Hour	Summary of Events and Information	Remarks and references to Appendices
Head quarters and No 4 Section VILLERS BROULIN	28th May	—	Reorganization continued	
	29th	—	do — do — rained all night	
No 1 + 3 Sections	30th	—	Drill. Raining in the morning.	
CAMBLIGNEUL				
No 2 Section ACQ	31st	—	Head quarters, No 2 Section + 2/3 No of No 4 Section marched to CAMBLIGNEUL at 8.30 pm	
Ammunition Dump LE PENDU			The Reorganization was practically complete on 31st May	

AMBlack
Major
Comg 25th DAC

25th DIVISIONAL ARTILLERY

25th DIVISIONAL AMMUNITION COLUMN

J U N E   1 9 1 6

The officer in charge
D.A.G's office
           Base.   C.121

I forward herewith War Diary of this unit
for June 1916.

                         AM Block
1 7/16   Bt Col.
       Comg 25th D A C

Army Form C. 2118.

Vol 9
June

WAR DIARY
or
INTELLIGENCE SUMMARY. 25th MAC

(Erase heading not required.)

Instructions regarding War Diaries and Intelligence
Summaries are contained in F. S. Regs., Part II.
and the Staff Manual respectively. Title pages
will be prepared in manuscript.

Place	Date	Hour	Summary of Events and Information	Remarks and references to Appendices
Head quarters	June 1916			
	1st & 3rd		Fine days - On the evening of the 2nd the remainder of No 4 Section marched & joined	
Nos 1,2,3 & 4 Section at			VILLIERS BRULIN & CAMBLIGNEUL - All surplus ordnance stores was returned to A.O.D	
CAMBLIGNEUL	4th		at Selongy.	
	5th		Fair weather	
H.Q. at			Fine in the middle, showery. S.W. wind light. 1 officer & 84 O.R. detached as a working party	
Nr. II LENS			for XVII th Corps. Heavy Artillery - having D.A.C. very short of men - Reinforcement of	
FRANCE	6th		28 O.R. arrived from Base	
1/100,000			Received 63 mules today, of a good class	
	7		Fine but cold -	
	8		Rained heavily night of 8/9.	
	9		Fine	
	10		Thunderstorm, heavy rain.	
	11		Cold, thundery rainy - a case of glanders have to & 2 Sections, all horses in D.A.C. to be	
			totally evacuated. This horse was one of the completes left at ABBEVILLE	
	12		rainy & cold	
	13		Cold weather. Remount horses took on this work. Malleining of horses commenced with No 1 Section	
			Machine shop for furniture, A.W. mech - Examination of No 1 & 3 Section & Head Quarters - malleining of No 2	
	14		Section	

Army Form C. 2118.

WAR DIARY
or
INTELLIGENCE SUMMARY. 25th V.A.C.

(Erase heading not required.)

Instructions regarding War Diaries and Intelligence Summaries are contained in F. S. Regs., Part II. and the Staff Manual respectively. Title pages will be prepared in manuscript.

Place	Date	Hour	Summary of Events and Information	Remarks and references to Appendices
Hedgedin 1,2,3 & 4 Section	15th June		Malleing continued. No 4 Section finished. No 1 & 3 Section present. 3 thankful centers in each section. C/110 returned their horses here as they had no use of [?]lenders, horses trireplace them found from No 1 & 3 Section. No 1 Section 101 horses. No 3 Section 13.	
CAMBLIGNEUL Ap. Sup. No 11 LENS FRANCE 1/100,000	16th June		Four remained. No 1 Section (Horses that came from C/110) inspected today. No 2 Section [?] at pretty bar, 1 unfit number	
	17th June		No 11 Section finally passed out. Filley in section, one horse shot & garden in retailer	
	18th June		Five hot eaten dulls. Horses that came from C/110 [?] fairly [?]. 7 horses which almost finished centers. about R. 57. Mobile Veterinary Section + 5 Veterinary Orius - all the horse standings [?] with Brick dust + horses put up [?] thousand of Brouls. border having to all upstand. our horses that taken for panel debility maderness. 3 aching horses + 53 under concert today, about 1 pm, but afternoon Gold, and W. morning.	
	19th		March to HUNT EN TERNOIS at 8 pm. Water for horses 3 miles away	
	20th		Cold, with W.	
	21st		marched to NEUVILLETTE at 8.30 pm. making horses shoes 3 miles away	
	22nd		marched to CANAPLES at 6 pm. undead horses to send at HEM for making place.	
	23rd 24th 25th		Remained at CANAPLES - No 1, 2 +3 Sections turnedaulked. No 4 Section in billets in H.Q. No 25th Mor R.A. Ser. H.Q. arrived + H.Q. left to conceale billets + barracks	
	26th 27th 28th		26th King came this afternoon + evening, 27 + 28 showers at intervals marched to CONTAY billets nay contalog. Rain throughout Potrnoon. Heavy rain most of the march	

Army Form C. 2118.

WAR DIARY
of
INTELLIGENCE SUMMARY. 25th T.M.C.

(Erase heading not required.)

Instructions regarding War Diaries and Intelligence Summaries are contained in F.S. Regs., Part II and the Staff Manual respectively. Title pages will be prepared in manuscript.

Place	Date	Hour	Summary of Events and Information	Remarks and references to Appendices
H.Q. 1st Section CONTAY	29th June		Halted at CONTAY - Fine - 6 horses + 15 O.R. transferred from No 1, 2 + 3 Sections to No. 110, 111 + 112 Brigades	
Gp No 11 LENS FRANCE 1 100000	30th June		Halt Contay - 25th BHQ. Came into CONTAY today - Brigades + OHC under 2 hours notice - 13 Remounts arrived. 9 O.R. from base arrived. Fine. Nothing of any military importance occurred during the past month which concerned the 25th T.M.C.	

MMBlack
Bt Lt Col
Comg 25th T.M.C.

31/7/16

2353 Wt. W2544/1454 700,000 5/15 D.D.&L. A.D.S.S./Forms/C. 2118.

WAR DIARY

25th DIVISION AMMUNITION COLUMN.

J U L Y

1 9 1 6

Army Form C. 2118.

July
Vol 10

WAR DIARY
or
INTELLIGENCE SUMMARY. 25ᵗʰ D.A.C.

(Erase heading not required.)

Instructions regarding War Diaries and Intelligence
Summaries are contained in F. S. Regs., Part II.
and the Staff Manual respectively. Title pages
will be prepared in manuscript.

Place	Date	Hour	Summary of Events and Information	Remarks and references to Appendices
Hedauville	1ˢᵗ July		Fine. Rendezvous 1. Letter arrived. Holders at CONTAY	
Sect 1,2,3&4 Sect CONTAY	2ⁿᵈ July		Fine. 11 Remounts received today — 4 Hoppers tendering 5720 to 5 Welsh Grenadier, 4 days to entrainp. 2 officers & 135 men of W/25 Tank Ambces arrived & passed to 32 Brit Dump & rest BOUZINCOURT	
Div Amm Park LENS	3ʳᵈ July		Fine day. Warmer. Rain at night	
100 eoe	4ᵗʰ July		Dull morning. Thunder & rain during the day – 2ⁿᵈ Lt F. A. BOWER arrived in exchange for Lt WINDER from 158ᵗʰ Bgde R.F.A. Remainder of T.M. Battery left for the Dumps – 1-2 & 3 Sections March Freight at 5, 6.30 + 9 p.m. for Ammn Dumps near BOUZINCOURT – 2ⁿᵈ Echn to 32ⁿᵈ Bde Ammn Park dump at 7.30 p.m.	
D.A.C. at WARLOY BOUZINCOURT	5ᵗʰ July		WARLOY. Wakes out. S.E. of BOUZINCOURT on the BOUZINCOURT – ALBERT rd. Headquarters & 2 Section about ½ mile S.E. of BOUZINCOURT. No 2 & 3 Section ½ mile N.W. of BOUZINCOURT. Dump ½ mile S.E.p BOUZINCOURT. 1.O.10.O.R. at AUTHUILLE grenade dump. 10 + 10 a.R at CRUCIFIX Corner about ½ mile No of AVELUY also a grenade dump. 5 officers joined D.A.C. today – 2nd Lt ARTHUR, GLIDDEAN + MEINDS. Damp day. Funeral Bombardment. Heavy bombardment last night – Fine day.	
Bt echn WARLOY	6ᵗʰ July		Dull morning, Rained in the afternoon + evening – Very quiet in enemy movement.	
	7ᵗʰ July		Rained all day. Received some ammunition late in the evening. Enemy dropped bombs on Shell imb BOUZINCOURT & killed one officer + 4 men wounded 1 officer (Capt ROBERTS D.A.D.O.S.)	

2353 Wt W2544/1454 700,000 5/15 D. D. & L.   A.D.S.S./Forms/C. 2118.

Army Form C. 2118.

WAR DIARY
or
INTELLIGENCE SUMMARY. 25 D.A.C.

(Erase heading not required.)

Instructions regarding War Diaries and Intelligence Summaries are contained in F. S. Regs., Part II. and the Staff Manual respectively. Title pages will be prepared in manuscript.

Place	Date	Hour	Summary of Events and Information	Remarks and references to Appendices
BOUZINCOURT	8th July		Fine day, warm + bright. A general strong wind shifted yesterday in the most hot & dry places.	
			Lt. BURGESS to ALBERT.	
	9th July		Fine day, nothing to report. Ammunition supply being carried on. Roads being shifted 400 yards they want.	
			Lt. Col. ALBERT.	
	10th July		Fine day, nothing to report.	
	11th "		" " " "	
	12th "		Tuesday. HASSARD + WYLD reported. 41 L. Donville received. 2 gutter accident of damage.	
	13th July		Heavy rain in the morning. Fine day.	
	14th "		Fine " nothing to report.	
	15th "		do - do.	
	16			
	17		Dull, showers at intervals.	
	18		Cooler. S.A.A. column of O.M.C. joined infantry Brigades of 25 Division in the evening 18 wagons from 4 Section, Remainder of O.M.C. arrived at Bouzincourt	
			not moving first afternoon but did N. road. nothing to report.	
	19th		Fine. Lt. HASSARD transferred to 110 Brigade.	
	20		Fine. 5 Officers + 110.O.R. arrived today from the Base.	
			2nd Lt. GARDINER, THOMSON. J.S. posted 112 Bde. VOSS. W.T. MARTIN transferred 112 Bde.	
			KBAY, G.A. posted to 111 Bde.	
	21		Fine day. N.E.N.E. wind.	
	22nd -24th		Wind N.E. East + N.E. generally fine, nothing to report affecting O.P.C.	

Army Form C. 2118.

WAR DIARY
or
INTELLIGENCE SUMMARY. 25th D.A.C.

(Erase heading not required.)

Instructions regarding War Diaries and Intelligence Summaries are contained in F. S. Regs., Part II. and the Staff Manual respectively. Title pages will be prepared in manuscript.

Place	Date	Hour	Summary of Events and Information	Remarks and references to Appendices
BOUZINCOURT	25th		Fine weather, N.E wind slight	
	26th		N.E wind, slight, hazy	
	27th		Misty morning, E wind. Fine day, warmer	
	28th		Fine - E wind, warm. Enemy dropped about 20 shells into BOUZINCOURT, not much damage done	
	29th		Fine a lot — probably 4.1 gun	
	30th		Fine, hot weather	
	31st		Wind very light from N.E. During the past month the D.A.C. was employed in ammunition supply. The one ammunition column at a dump at BOUZINCOURT received from Main Dump at PUCHEVILLERS. All ammunition was brought from railhead to dump & from thence to dump of Brigade Ammunition. About 6 Fair where the work was very well. Ammunition was brought from railhead to dump at a dump of Brigade Ammunition and to Fair where the work was heavy. The D.A.C. began to keep a team of 150 men employed taking supplies & small arms ammunition. The 4 section received at D.D.D.S. men employed taking supplies & small arms ammunition to be supplied to HARLEY from there on other wagons carrying - 20 wagons a day while held the supply to HARLEY from there on other wagons carrying kept clear of supplies. All ammunition arrangements worked very well & the dumps were always found arrangements worked very satisfactorily & I consider the casualties from wounds during the month nil	

Murdoch Br Col
Comy 25 D.A.C.
31/7/16

2353 Wt. W2544/1454 700,000 5/15 D. D. & L. A.D.SS./Forms/C. 2118.

25th Divisional Artillery

25th DIVISIONAL AMMUNITION COLUMN

AUGUST 1 9 1 6

Army Form C. 2118.

Vol 11

WAR DIARY
or
INTELLIGENCE SUMMARY. 25th D.A.C.

(Erase heading not required.)

Place	Date	Hour	Summary of Events and Information	Remarks and references to Appendices
Bouzincourt Head qrs 1, 2 & 3 Sections No 4 Section WARLOY Reference map No 11 LENS FRANCE 1/10000	Aug 1st		Fine hot day – about 1 p.m. 4 German aeroplanes came over & though fired at by anti-aircraft guns went right over the lines	
	Aug 2nd	About 3 a.m.	The enemy dropped about 18 shells from 4" gun into the village, heavy damage apps to house of No 1 Section town – One 9.5" wagon of No 1 Section blown up, 4 bays wounded, another shell dropped in "Hotel yards". Three fires within 4 yards of a hose, but did no damage. One shell dropped about a yard from a motor car belonging to Heavy artillery had parked, which a bomb. Sadler CALVERT was wounded by accident and to Hospital – shifted Head quarters & No 1 Section camps in the evening, a few hundred yards to the EAST of the dumps. Sadler CALVERT died this evening.	
	August 3rd		Fine weather, hot. The new dumps were formed unsatisfactory, the road not being to narrow for motor traffic, a new position was chosen selected north of the — road junction about a mile east of SENLIS S of SENLIS on HEDAUVILLE – BOUZINCOURT	
	August 4		Moved H.Q. & dumps from position could not more certain army transport parks. S.S. Pte. WILLIAMS 20 Section wounded by shell fire whilst... — 2nd day Cholera. No 3 Section Wt.b4.631 Q morley or "" horse wounded in same fire from him, horse to hospital	
	August 5th		Fine day. whilst during the night to 1 Section "mollerines" today – BOUZINCOURT Enemy dropped some shells in BOUZINCOURT killing No 50789 Drain DAYMEN. No 2 Section	
	August 6th		Fine day. No 2 Section moved camp to a camp near the dumps	
	August 7th		Both camps shelled by f. fire... No shells by 1 Section moved the camps near the dumps. Fine afternoon	
	August 8th		Fine day. Enemy dropped some shells about ½ a mile away.	

Army Form C. 2118.

WAR DIARY
or
INTELLIGENCE SUMMARY.   25th AC.
(Erase heading not required.)

Instructions regarding War Diaries and Intelligence Summaries are contained in F.S. Regs., Part II. and the Staff Manual respectively. Title pages will be prepared in manuscript.

Place	Date	Hour	Summary of Events and Information	Remarks and references to Appendices
Head quarters camp at	9th August		Fine hot day.	
	10th August		Seen in the morning. Local round. BOUZINCOURT was shelled during the afternoon	
Bet. between Section between BOUZINCOURT & SENLIS			+ evening. Fine afternoon. No 2016 Capt CAMPBELL # - h 10 SI/SS No PALMER F.- 67251 5 SI/M/SS WT was wounded by shellfire in BOUZINCOURT. RT. BOUZINCOURT shelled in the morning + ground about ½ mile west	
	11		Heavy mist in the morning. BOUZINCOURT shelled in the morning.	
			off H.Q. O.A.C. camp.	
No 3 Section	12		Fine day – quiet round here, or horse of H.Q. D.A.C. destroyed, broke leg from kick	
between BOUZINCOURT	13		Fine, round chapel + S.W.	
MILLENCOURT			S.W. round around at intervals all day. Rained very heavy, especially somewhere East.	
No 4 Section at	15		Fine but all – S.W. round around.	
	16		Fine S.W. BOUZINCOURT shelled the evening about 8pm – approximately 8 in kmshts	
	17		Fine S.W.	
WARLOY	18		Fine day and evening K.N. – troops impractical for lorries	
	19		Rain early morning S.W. round – troops impractical for lorries, arrangements made for watching the order of the road.	
Reference Sheet 44.11 LENS	20		Fine morning – W.mm – enemy dropped 3 shells into BOUZINCOURT about 7.45pm	
FRANCE 1/100,000	21		Fine day – ordinary work. Began a shop – 10.2 fuzes issued into 4.45.5 Block to R.F. worth guns.	

2353 Wt. W2344/1451 700,000 5/15 D.D.&L.   A.D.S.S./Forms/C. 2118.

WAR DIARY
or
INTELLIGENCE SUMMARY. 23rd D.A.C.
(Erase heading not required.)

Army Form C. 2118.

Place	Date	Hour	Summary of Events and Information	Remarks and references to Appendices
Dd Bapaume	22nd		Fine day. — Dumps were shelled today by enemy, two fell on the dump itself, 2 or 3 more	
Dumps at Headquarters at V36 10.5	23rd		near the position S.19. about 7.30 p.m. major Thompson + H.Q. of 23rd D.A.C. visited nr 22.6. O.H.M.L. W.S. slightly wounded in face with debris from shell. Telephonic communication dumps at the rail-place, commenced today. Dark, outstandingly as dry weather. Three enemy airplanes were seen over enemy trenches.	
MAP 57.D	24th		Fine morning, rain during night. S.E. wind very slight.	
FRANCE 40000	25th		Dull. — S.W. Rain at times.	
	26th		S.W. overcast, rain at times.	
nr HEDAUVILLE	27		S.W. Heavy showers at intervals.	
-WARLOY	28		do. — finer in the evening. S.A.A. section of No 1 Section + transport to 4 Section. Capt WYLD took over position S.A.A. dumps from 48th D.G. at Y.M.C.A. welcome arrival of troops E end. Thunderstorm in afternoon, afterwards rain. 11 E.D.A.C. (No 2 Section)	
Nos 1, 2, + 3 Sections in area noted	29		Rain morning. fine later. Gone in to be supplied from ourdumps.	
	30		S.W. wind. fair.	
	31st		Fine N.W. wind slight. nothing to report.	

A.M. [signature]
Major
Army 23rd D.A.C.

25th. DIVISION

25th. DIVISION AMMUNITION COLUMN.

SEPTEMBER

1 9 1 6.

Army Form C. 2118.

Vol 12

WAR DIARY
or
INTELLIGENCE SUMMARY. 25th D.T.C.

(Erase heading not required.)

Instructions regarding War Diaries and Intelligence Summaries are contained in F. S. Regs., Part II. and the Staff Manual respectively. Title pages will be prepared in manuscript.

Place	Date	Hour	Summary of Events and Information	Remarks and references to Appendices
V.14.a.0.5.	1st September		Fine day – N.W. wind. light B4 & B6 the supplied with ammunition from dump – h.3 sector	
& HEDAUVILLE			18th D.T.C. statute for test purposes.	
WARLOY Rd	2nd & 3rd		nil	
dump 57 D	4th		This morning shells were dropped at 3am. East of SENLIS and in the vicinity of FORCEVILLE	
FRANCE			This afternoon the ridge East of SENLIS was again shelled – 18th D.T.C. ceased drawing ammunition from the dump.	
1 WOODS	5th		nil	
	6th		1st GILFILLAN & Y.25. T.M.B. – 2nd HARRISON from T.M.B4 & 25th D.T.C	
Head quarters	7th		2nd HAYDEN to 112th T.M.B – 11th D.T.C. moved and drew ammunition from our dump for next day. Remainder of aircraft very active over our area – 2 bombs dropped apparently in the HEDAUVILLE dump – 2 horses recovered, no had the alert (not having other hurt)	
No dump a0 above –	8th		BOUZINCOURT dump shelled last night by the enemy & by that about 10 pm. — a few rounds of small calibre came out from German lines with heavy gas ? (?) 11 shrapnel fell in a number of small villages and fine German lines with	
No. 1, 2 & 3			apparently in the 17 minute, apparently directed to the French with a view to enemy dumps.	
Sedan dump	9th		nil	
on the road	10th		nil	
	11th		nil	
No 4 Sector	12th		Our 60rd Artillery went into the "bus" again this morning – two labelled ammunition supply	
at WARLOY			2nd Lt Gardiner took charge of dump – 10 wagons from No 1, 2 & 3 Sector & 20 more from No 4 Sector with exceptions.	
	13th		nil	
	14th		nil	
	15th		nil	
	16th			

WAR DIARY
or
INTELLIGENCE SUMMARY. 25th S.A.C.

(Erase heading not required.)

Army Form C. 2118.

Place	Date	Hour	Summary of Events and Information	Remarks and references to Appendices
Headquarters 1.2.3.&4 Sections as before	17 Sept 1914		Lt TACON & 5 O.R. & AULT Red return.	
	18"		} 2nd - small expenditure of ammunition	
	19"		}	
	20 September		22 O.R. arrived from the Base.	
	21st		W. 25 T.M. Battery attached for adm - 20 men of Bn Battery detailed to work w. the troops, rations, from the M.T. section	
	22"		nil	
	23rd		nil	
	24"		Some shells dropped in Wh Valley N of HEDAUVILLE	
	25"		5 enemy aeroplanes seen over the camp about 11 am - 6 officers reported to staff from the base. 2nd Lt BRIGGS & No 2 Section & CURLEWIS & No 4 This evening option two only are posted to D.A.C. Section - Lt WYLD posted to Nº 2 "Brigade.	
	26"		Received orders to relieve F KOUZINCOOPT, W 25 T.M.B. Cases to T.M.C. Brigade away.	
	27		nil	
	28		nil	
	29		nil	
	30			

A.W. Black
Lt Col
Comm 25th S.A.C.

25th DIVISIONAL ARTILLERY

25th DIVISIONAL AMMUNITION COLUMN

OCTOBER   1916

Vol XIV

Army Form C. 2118.

Vol 13

WAR DIARY
or
INTELLIGENCE SUMMARY. 25th D.T.C.

(Erase heading not required.)

Place	Date	Hour	Summary of Events and Information	Remarks and references to Appendices
Headquarters 1, 2 & 3 Sections at BOUZINCOURT — ALBERT Road	1st Nov 1916		Head Quarters & No 1, 2, & 3 Sections moved to camps on BOUZINCOURT — ALBERT road. Dumps were to practice formerly occupied by 18th D.T.C. S.A.A. & Grenade Dumps taken over from 11th D.T.C at V.17.c.6.6 on SENLIS—MILLENCOURT road. 2nd Lt GARDNER in charge of dumps. S.G.S. & 2 L.G.S. dumps from east of AVELUIN section and 6 O.S dumps from No 4 Section. Total 85 men G.S. lorries, this includes 22 infantry (on detaching bomb. 2nd Lt BALL & 2nd Lt JOHNSON in charge of dumps) other personnel transferred from 112th Bde. 2nd Lt GARDNER transferred 2nd Lt JOHNSTON was transferred from 112th Bde via 2nd Lt GARDNER to 112th Brigade — and 2nd Lt JOHNSTON (with ammo dump (S.A.A.)	
Dump No 2 2nd Section Map 57 O Item 40000 4th Section at WARLEY	2nd 3rd 7th 8th 9,10,11 12th	6am	and N.C. Enemy dropped some shell shot 300 to 600 yards away from H.Q camp. All rounds with 20ct. Probably 4.2". Hrs were from 5pm to 6pm. and 113th Bde R.F.A reports, They have the supplies by no such ammunition. The transport of rations to this artillery has our the carried out by the D.T.C. — 20 G.S. wagons from no 4 section are employed on this duty.	

Army Form C. 2118.

WAR DIARY
or
INTELLIGENCE SUMMARY.   25th L.A.C.

(Erase heading not required.)

Place	Date	Hour	Summary of Events and Information	Remarks and references to Appendices
In the Field	13th October		nil	
	14th October		nil	
	15th October		Corpl. Davis (W.11770) & Pte. 1085 Andrew MAHON were taken on strength on arrival whilst attached to 113 Trench Mortar Battery	
	16th October		Colonel Block R.S.A. proceeded on Leave. Capt. G.H. Gaurton was on ward	
	17th October		Draft of 33 O.R. joined from Base, posted to Sections	
	19th October		Lieut G.E. TOMARON posted to W/25 Heavy T.M.B.	
	20th October		Night of 20th-21st about 2am. Shots fell in the vicinity of H.Q. & No. 1 Section. Pieces were all only	
			No casualties. Also several pieces fell on the church.	
	21st October		M.O.R. Faulkner to Brigade	
	22nd October		Lt. Capt. L.N. Elliot returned from Base	
	23rd October		Orders to D.Coy etc. from L.N. Drury for 52nd Div. dumps opened & abolition of W.13.c.5.7.	
	24th October		5 N.C.Os posted from Base - posted to Section	
	25th October		66 O.R. joined from Base posted to Section. 86 remounts joined from Base, posted to Sections	
	26th October		45 remounts posted to Brigade	
	27th October		52 O.R. posted to Brigade. Col Block returned from Leave & resumed command. Capt. Byrnes Avis	
	28th October		granted 2 leave	
			nil	
	29th October		nil	
	30th			
	31st		14 O.R. joined from base.	

AM Block
Maj
Comg 25th OMC

25th DIVISIONAL ARTILLERY

25th DIVISIONAL AMMUNITION COLUMN

NOVEMBER 1916

Page 1

Army Form C. 2118.

WAR DIARY
or
INTELLIGENCE SUMMARY. 2 S.D.A.C.
(Erase heading not required.)

Vol. IV November

Instructions regarding War Diaries and Intelligence Summaries are contained in F.S. Regs. Part II. and the Staff Manual respectively. Title pages will be prepared in manuscript.

Place	Date 1916	Hour	Summary of Events and Information	Remarks and references to Appendices
Headquarters	November 1st		nil	
Sections 1, 2 & 3	November 2nd		nil	
Section —	November 3rd		nil	
BOUZINCOURT	November 4th		23 O.R. transferred to Brigade.	
— ALBERT Road	November 5th		nil	
nr BOUZINCOURT No 4 Section	November 6th		about 9.30 pm large enemy aeroplane & explosions seen due South, presumed by the enemy. The about 6 miles away; explosions continued during the night, about 11.30 am Telegram received that Zeppelin' had been seen moving back over FRICOURT	
nr WARLOY Refuses Major	November 7th	at 10.20 pm	2nd Lt. M. WHITEFORD reported for wounded for DONNETS POST command. to No 2 Section — 2nd Lt. WARD transferred from 40th D.A.C. unreported to No 2 Section. 2nd Lt. E. SHAW reported arrival fr 336 13th RFA posted to No 1 Section 2nd Lt. J.H.S.E. FLINT " " 2 Section	
No 11 LENS	November 8th		enemy Zeppelin was not SENLIS abt 9.37 am at 17.0.1.R arrived from Base	
100000	November 9th		Great aerial activity in AS morning 2nd Lt. W. WATKINSON arrived	
	November 10th		17th D.A.C. posted to No 3 Section — also to report changes gains	
	November 11th		1 O.R. reported arrival from Base. nil	
	November 12th		5 O.R. arrived from Base	
	November 13th		Last night enemy dropped a few shells in the district of SENLIS. 2nd Lt. JOHNSTON admitted to Hospital suffering from Jaundice.	

2353 Wt. W25141/1454 700,200 5/15 D. D. & L. A.D.S.S./Forms/C. 2118.

Army Form C. 2118.

WAR DIARY
or
INTELLIGENCE SUMMARY.

25th D.A.C.
November
Vol X 5

(Erase heading not required.)

Place	Date	Hour	Summary of Events and Information	Remarks and references to Appendices
	14th Nov 1915		nil	
	15 Nov		Some bombs dropped on WARLOY between 1 - 1.30 a.m. by aeroplane. Some H.V. gun shrapnel shot ½ mile East of our H.Q. Camp. Some shells from H.V. gun	
	16th Nov		Enemy aeroplane seen early in morning. Shots at him by antiaircraft between this sleepers & throwing Mini but stops against the aeroplane which is evidently flown up from the ground. Some form of light engine much in use. Infantry, 2 am & 3 am by aeroplanes, much about.	
	17" "		Many bombs dropped this morning. Lieut TACON went to Hospital this morning. Country vigorously assaulted. B.S.M. ROLFE No 2 Section shot himself this morning.	
	18th "		nil	
	19th "		nil	
	20" "		nil	
	21" "		Received orders that the 25th Divisional Artillery would move on the 23rd, all ammunition from A to be loaded over to 11th Brigade, including S.A.A. & Grenades. Wagons to move empty. Handing over ammunition.	
	22nd Nov		Commenced S.A.A. dump closed. Lt adjutant MILLER returned from leave. 25 mule convoy from Renescure reached No 1 Section.	
	23rd Nov		Marched at 7.30 am to ORVILLE via ACHEUX - LOUVENCOURT - MARIEUX arrived about 1 pm. H.Q. & No 3 at 7.30 - No 4 from WARLOY at 7.30 - No 2 at 8 - No 1 at 8.30 - Farm Billets, 18 miles	
	24th Nov		No Section at 9 - H.Q. & No 2 at 9.50 - No 3 at 10.30. 06.4 at 10.30 marched to VACQUERIE-LE-BOCQ via DOULLENS-FREVENT and LIGNY-SUR-CANCHE - H.Q. arrived about 4 pm - very bad & insufficient billets. 17 miles	
	25th Nov		marched to VALHUON - 13 miles - No 4 - 10.30 - No 2 - 11 am - No 3 & H.Q. 11.30 am - No 1 12 noon - H.Q. arrived 4.45 pm. Good billets but horse lines	
	26th Nov		Halted at VALHUON	

Page 3

Army Form C. 2118.

WAR DIARY
or
INTELLIGENCE SUMMARY.   25th A.T.C.   November   Vol XV

(Erase heading not required.)

Instructions regarding War Diaries and Intelligence Summaries are contained in F. S. Regs., Part II. and the Staff Manual respectively. Title pages will be prepared in manuscript.

Place	Date	Hour	Summary of Events and Information	Remarks and references to Appendices
VALHUON	27th November		Halted to-day.	
LIGNY-LES-AIRE	28th November		Marched to LIGNY-LES-AIRE via PERNES - FERFAY - AUCHY-AUX-BOIS. No 2 Section at 9.30 am - No 1 at 10am - No 4 at 10.30am - H.Q + No 3 at 11am - H.Q arrived about 4pm. Distance about 12 miles - 2.0.R arrived from Pro Bau	
THIENNES	29th November		Marched to THIENNES via LAMBRES & AIRE. No 3 Section + H.Q at 10am - No 4 at 10.15am - No 1 at 10.30am - No 2 at 10.45am - H.Q arrived about 2pm. Distance 10 miles.	
Le ROURLOSHUL	30th November		Marched to Le ROURLOSHUL via STEENBECQUE - HAZEBROUCK - STRAZEELE - FLETRE. H.Q + No 1 Section 9.45am No 3 at 10am No 2 at 10.15am No 4 at 10.30am head of column arrived about 4pm about 13 miles.	

Animals arrived generally speaking in good condition especially the mules although the frost which has been continuous to 10th ult - 345 hrs, had a good effect on the heavy mules. Heart transport gradually attaining the demands made of a deficit.

AMBlack
Major
Comdg 25th A.T.C.

25th DIVISIONAL ARTILLERY

25th DIVISIONAL AMMUNITION COLUMN

DECEMBER 1916

Army Form C. 2118.

WAR DIARY
or
INTELLIGENCE SUMMARY. 25th D.A.C.

(Erase heading not required.)

Instructions regarding War Diaries and Intelligence Summaries are contained in F. S. Regs., Part II. and the Staff Manual respectively. Title pages will be prepared in manuscript.

Place	Date	Hour	Summary of Events and Information	Remarks and references to Appendices
Hunstanton	18th Dec	—	nil	
"	19	—	exchange 12 hundred O Strays for 12 S.A.A. Each belonging to Regimental Reserve from each Brigade	
B9 c1	20	—	received 34 A vehicles	
No 1 Section				
B 23 C 22	21	" 8a.m.	Detachment from 25th Division were inspected by the G.O.C. in C.	
No 2 Section	22	" "	nil	
		" "	nil	
B 14 a 63	23		nil	
No 3 Section	24	"	55 command's arrived	
	25	—	nil	
B 8 b 15		—	nil	
No 4 Section	26		nil	
	27		3.O.R. arrived from base (Sergeant ?, 1 full ?? his pair 2 L.K.A. 2 without ?)	
B 14 c 96	28		nil	
	29		nil	
Gun amm dump	30		Lt A. DEWAR arrived in Europe from R.F.C. posted to No 1 Section	
B 11 6 20	31st		nil	
Grenade dump				
18 53 37				
Ref Map Sheet				
36 N.W				
FRANCE				
1/20000				

[signature] Bt Col
31/12/15 Comg 25th D.A.C.

To D A G
    G.H.Q.
        3rd Echelon.

Herewith War Diary of 25th Div Amn Col.
for Month of January 1917
Reference your   C.R./140/452 of 22.2.17

                    Fitzgerald Cust
                    for
10.3.17   B. Gen. CRA. 25th Div.

25

Army Form C. 2118.

WAR DIARY
or
INTELLIGENCE SUMMARY. 23rd D.A.C.

(Erase heading not required.)

Vol 10

Instructions regarding War Diaries and Intelligence Summaries are contained in F. S. Regs., Part II. and the Staff Manual respectively. Title pages will be prepared in manuscript.

Place	Date	Hour	Summary of Events and Information	Remarks and references to Appendices
Headquarters	1st	nil	nil	
B9C81	2nd	nil	nil	
No 1 Section at	3rd		18. O.R. arrived from the Base	
B 23 c 22	4th		2nd Lt. W. S. E. FLINT & Lt G. E. JONARON transferred to 36th Division. 2nd Lt. DEWAR left	
Headquarters			Gun ammunition Dump	
B 14 a 63	5th		2nd Lt A. WARD transferred to 36th Division	
No 3 Section	6th		nil	
B 8 G 15	7th		nil	
No 4 Section	8th		No 2 Section army Forage Reserve transferred to horse lines. New camp as per horse area	
B 14 C 96			cleared of by the Veterinary Officer.	
Gun Ammn	9th		Q. M. S. PETTIGREW arrived from Base, posted to No 3 Section	
Dump at	10th		nil	
B 118 20	11th		5. O. R. arrived from Base	
	12th		2/Lt BARNES went to Grenade Dump flats our from 2nd Lt SHAW	
Grenade +	13th		Lt T.D. BARNES took over Grenade Dump. 2nd Lieut E.T.F. HARRISON met with Hospital	
S.A.A. Dump	14th		2nd Lt E. SHAW proceeded to 2nd Army Artillery School & Corporal MASON to 1st Sec Tour	
B E 637	15th		nil	
Ext maps	16th		2nd Lt J.W. SHARMAN 23820 Corporal J. LEAR to 4 Section, 78147 Pt T. DUFFY to 2 Section 367256	
sheet 36 NW			H. McELHINEY to Section went to T.M. School at BERETHEN	
FRANCE	17th		nil	
1	18th		nil	
20000	19th		Captain B.M. COLLARD R.A.M.C. returned to ENGLAND on expiration of 2 years service.	

JANUARY 1917

#353 Wt. W2544/1454 700,000 5/15 D. D. & L. A.D.S.S./Forms/C. 2118.

Army Form C. 2118.

WAR DIARY
or
INTELLIGENCE SUMMARY.   25th J.F.C.

(Erase heading not required.)

Instructions regarding War Diaries and Intelligence Summaries are contained in F. S. Regs., Part II. and the Staff Manual respectively. Title pages will be prepared in manuscript.

Place	Date	Hour	Summary of Events and Information	Remarks and references to Appendices
In Billets	20th	—	10. O.R. arrived and posted to Section. 2nd Lt ATKINSON went to Hospital	
	21st		nil	
	22nd		nil	
	23rd		nil	
	24th		nil	
	25th	—	Lt J. BLAIR, G.A. McDOWELL & 2nd Lt H.K. BANKS joined and were posted to No 3, 4 & 1 Section respectively	
	26th		nil	
	27th		nil	
	28th		nil	
	29th		nil	
	30th		nil	
	31st		2nd Lt J. W. SHARMAN R.C.O. and returned from T.M Course	

JANUARY 1917

C.W.Block
BGC
Comdg 25th J.F.C.

31/1/17

Page 1

Army Form C. 2118.

WAR DIARY
or
INTELLIGENCE SUMMARY. 25th D.A.C.

(Erase heading not required.)

February 1917

Volume XVIII

Vol 17

Place	Date	Hour	Summary of Events and Information	Remarks and references to Appendices
	February 1917			
Headquarters	1st	—	2nd Lt H. BALL & 5 O.R. went to T.M. school at BERTHEN	
B9 c81	2nd	—	Nil.	
No 1 Section	3rd	—	Nil	
B 23 C 22	4th	—	Col. A. H. BLOCK proceed on leave. CAPT G.H. FRASER took over command	
No 2 Section	5th	—	Nil.	
park at B14 a 63	6th	—	Nil	
	7th	—	Nil	
park at B23 C.53	8th	—	Nil	
No 3 Section	9th	—	Nil 2nd Lt SHAW returned from 2nd Army School, Formery Cross. 2nd Lt BANKS & 2 O.R. went to Army School	
B8 c-15	10th	—	Nil	
No 4 Section	11th	—	2nd Conf TRENCHARD joined from 16th R.D. & Arty. posted to No 4 Sect.	
B14 c96	12th	—	Re-organization of 25th D.A.C. completed. No 1 & 3 Sect. completed to establishment from No 2 Sect. No 2 Sect. form nucleus of A.F.B.A.C. under Col. L.N.ECLIOT 25th D.A.C.	
Pt. FRANCE Sheet 36.N.W			Now composed as follows No 1 Sect. No 1.5. & 2 Sect. (No 3 Sect ola No. 3) "B" soldier No 3 Sect. (ola No.4). Less 3 B.S. wagons. Case 3 B.S. wagons, 15 animals. Pair in 4 gunners posted to	
Scale 1/20,000			No 2., 5 gunners posted to No. 1.	
gunners annum stumps B 11 b 20				
Grenade + Sap dump B 56 -37				

Page 2.

Army Form C. 2118.

WAR DIARY
or
INTELLIGENCE SUMMARY. 23rd W. D.A.C.

February 1917

(Erase heading not required.)

Place	Date	Hour	Summary of Events and Information	Remarks and references to Appendices
Headquarters B.9.C.81.	February 1917 13th		Nil	
	14th	—	N-Col. AH BLOCK returns from leave & resumes command. 2nd Lt H. BALL & 5 O.R. return from T.M. Corps	
	15th	"	nil	
	16th	"	nil	
	17th	"	3 4. O.R. posted to Brigades 10 + 16 O.R. joined from Base	
	18th	"	+ 2nd Lt. J. IRVINE-WATSON 2nd Lt H. BALL transferred 2nd Lt J. IRVINE-WATSON transferred to 110th Bty RFA to W.23. T.M. Battery. 2nd Lt SHARMAN transferred to W.25 T.M. Battery	
	19th	"		
	20th	"	nil	
	21st	"	nil	
	22nd	"	nil	
	23rd	"	nil	
	24th	"	3. O.R's arrived from Base	
	25th	"		
	26th	"	2nd Lt DEWAR transferred to W.25. T.M. Battery. 2nd Lt BALL returns to D.A.C.	
	27th	"	to EBBLINGHEM started at 9am, leading section arrived 4.15pm rear section at 6.20pm. distance about 22 miles — via BAILLEUL — CAESTRE & HONDEQUEM D.A.C. arrived K. SETQUES via ARQUES & WIZERNES distance about 12 miles. started at 9am leading section arrived 12.30pm. 2nd Lt A.A. WARD reported his arrival from Base. Lt 12 O.R. to 1 Section. Lt S.A. WEBB appointed 2nd command but before Lt Capts. C.H. FRASER commenced putting up overhead cover for horses of horses of the D.A.C.	
	28th	"		AHBlock Lt Col. Comy 25 DAC.

2353 Wt. W2544/1454 700,000 5/15 D. D. & L. A.D.S.S./Forms/C. 2118. 2B 2/17

March 1917

Army Form C. 2118.

Vol 18

WAR DIARY
of
INTELLIGENCE SUMMARY. 25th D.A.C.

(Erase heading not required.)

Place	Date MARCH.17	Hour	Summary of Events and Information	Remarks and references to Appendices
Headquarters Nos 1, 2 & 3 Sections at SETQUES (B)(4) map Sheet 5.a. HAZEBROUCK BELGIUM. 1/100,000	1st		Captain. A. WYLIE. R.A.M.C. joined the 25th D.A.C. for duty.	
	2nd		Captain. C.H. FRASER transferred to 112th Bde. R.F.A.	
	5th		Lt.Colonel C.S. HOPE-JOHNSTONE took over command of 25th D.A.C.	
	13th		2 O.R's joined from 1/23rd T.M.B.	
	18th		HORSE SHOW.	
	19th		2nd Lieut. W. ATKINSON rejoined.	
	19th		27. O.R's joined from R.H. & R.F.A. Base Depot, & were posted as follows :- 110th/33rd RFA. 10 112th/33rd RFA. 11 25th D.A.C. 6 – 27 Total.	
	21st		March. SETQUES to RACQUINGHEM. Area – about 11 miles –	
	22nd		March. RACQUINGHEM Area to CAUDESCURE (Neuf Berquin Area), about 17 miles. Nos 1 & 2 Sections started from Cohen-- HdQus & No 3 Sec: " Racquinghem – 9.30 a.m.	
	28th		March. CAUDESCURE to NEUF BERQUIN – (L.14.D.67. Sheet 36.A. 1/40,000) – No 1 Sector. S.S.W. of STEENWERCK – (A.22.d.3.9. Sheet 36. 1/40,000) – No 2 Sector. N. of ESTAIRES ~~E.S.E. of BAILLEUL~~ – (G.19.f.88. Sheet 36 1/40,000) } No 3. Sector. (L.17.d.23 Sheet 36A 1/40000) }	
	30th		March. NEUF BERQUIN to E.S.E. of BAILLEUL (S.22.a.11. Sheet 28. 1/40000) No 1. Sector. CAUDESCURE to N. of ESTAIRES (G.8.c.2.2. Sheet 36 1/40000) HdQrs. 25th D.A.C.	
	31st		1. O.R. joined from HdQo. R.A. 25th Divisin –	C.S. Hope-Johnstone
	31st		Captain W.C. SMITH (R.C. Chaplain) joined from home.	Lieut.Col. R.A.C. Commdg 25th D.A.C.

Army Form C. 2118.

WAR DIARY
25TH DIVISIONAL AMMUNITION COLUMN.
INTELLIGENCE SUMMARY.
(Erase heading not required.)

Instructions regarding War Diaries and Intelligence Summaries are contained in F.S. Regs., Part II. and the Staff Manual respectively. Title pages will be prepared in manuscript.

April 1917 — Page 1.
Vol 19

Place	Date 1917 APRIL	Hour	Summary of Events and Information	Remarks and references to Appendices
Cul-de-Sac, ESTAIRES	6th		2 Officers + 18 ORs joined from Base. ORs posted as follows:—	16. DAC. 1. 110th Bde. RFA. 1. 112th Bde. RFA.
"	8th		Move. Hd. Qrs. D.A.C. from G.8.C.2.2. (sheet 36) to A.2.2.d.9.2. (sheet 36). Gun Section. N°3 Section. from Z.17.d.2.3. (sheet 36A) " G.8.c.2.2. (sheet 36)(camp vacated by H°36 D.A.C.)	
"	9th		Captain B. PARKINS invalided to England.	
A.23.C.4. STEENWERCK	13th		10 Other Ranks joined from Base — ... D.A.C. (25th Dn.)	
"	24th		2 Lieut. A.A. Ward transferred to 36th Dn. ARTILLERY.	
"	30th		44 Other Ranks joined from Base — Posted as follows :—	16. 110th Bde. RFA. 23. 112th Bde. RFA. 5. D.A.C.

April 30th 1917.

C.S. Hope-Johnstone
Lieut Colonel.
Comdg. D.A.C., 25th Division.

May 1917

Army Form C. 2118.

WAR DIARY
or
INTELLIGENCE SUMMARY. 25th Div: Amm: Column.
(Erase heading not required.)

Vol 20

Place	Date	Hour	Summary of Events and Information	Remarks and references to Appendices
	1917			
	May 1st		NOTES. H.Q.Col. from A.25.a.22. (Sheet 36) to K.4.c.22. (Sheet 36 A)	
			" N°1 Sec. " S.22.a.1.1. (Sheet 28) " K.4.c.4.2. "	
			" N°2 Sec. " A.22.d.3.9. (Sheet 36) " E.28.a.2.2. (—)	
	May 3rd		MOVE. N°3. Sec. from L.23.b.2.2 (Sheet 36a) to E.29 Central (—)	
			" " " G.8.C.(Sh.36.Sec)(Sheet 36) " E.29 Central (—)	
	May 4th		POSTINGS. 3 O.Rs. Ranks - posted to Trench Mortars. 25th Division.	
	May 7th		POSTINGS. 8 " " " " "	
			2/Lieut W.F.N. Forrest. Transferred to R.F.C. (Balloon Section)	
	May 9th		MOVES. H.Q.Col. from K.4.c.22. (Sheet 36A) to T.25.a.8.2. (Sheet 28)	
			" N°1 Sec. " K.4.c.2.2. (—) " T.20.C.2.1. (—)	
			" N°2 Sec. " E.28.a.2.2 (—) " S.22.a.1.1. (—)	
			" N°3 Sec. " E.29 Central (—) " S.29 Central (—)	
	May 10th		POSTINGS. 70 other Ranks joined from Base - posted to 25th D.A.C.	
			5 " " " " " " posted to Trench Mortars - 25th Division.	
	May 11th		MOVE. N°1. Sec. from T.20.C.2.1. (Sheet 28) " S.23.a. 7.5. (Sheet 28)	
	May 14th		POSTINGS. 3 O.Rs. Ranks (mustering from draft on 10th instant) joined - posted to 2nd D.A.C.	
	May 16th		" 4 O.Rs. Ranks posted to 112th Bde R.F.A.	
	May 19th		Lieut. J.R.E. Trenchard: joined to 298th Army Field Artillery Brigade.	
	May 25th		2/Lieut. A. Flowers. joined from B.A.E. & appointed Adjutant. 25th D.A.C.	
	May 28th		CASUALTIES. N°1. Sec. Brs Fishwick. Hepworth, Walker, Waldron, & G/S Cleary, Carville (all wounded) vide CASUALTY RETURN
			" " N°2. Sec. B: Bagely - G/S Zantor (Killed) + Halm (wounded) (Gnr Gartico. No.1 Section)
			" " N°3. Sec. B: Fraser, G/S Cole + Kemp (Gas) - G/S Kingsford (Killed) (Gnr Gritten No.1 Section) 29/5/17 wounded
	May 29th		" " N°3. Sec. Br Hillery & Bdr Atwood (wounded) (Gnr Grisen No.1 Section) dated 29th May 1917. 30-5-17 Wounded)
	May 30th		NOTES. H.Q.Col. from T.20 a 8.2. (Sheet 28) to T.19. F.1.2. (Sheet 28)	
			" N°1 Sec. " S.23 a 7.5. (—)	
			" N°2 Sec. " S.22 a.1.1. (—)	
			" N°3 Sec. " S.29 Central (—)	

MAY 31st 1917.

C.S. Hope-Thrustal - Lieut. Colonel -

Comdg 25th D.A.C.

WAR DIARY or INTELLIGENCE SUMMARY.

Army Form C. 2118.

25th Div. Amm. Column.

Vol 21

Place	Date 1917 June	Hour	Summary of Events and Information	Remarks and references to Appendices
In the field	2nd		1 (R) Horse & 7 mules joined	
	6th		3 Other Ranks posted to Trench Mortar Batteries	
	7th		Move - 25th BAC - from 7.19. & 1.2. (Sheet 28) to S.12. & 7.7. (Sheet 28)	
	9th		1 (R) Horse - killed (Shellfire)	
	11th		33 Other Ranks joined - from RH & RFA Base Depot.	
	12th		2 Other Ranks wounded { 107850 Saddler Goulding. R (severely wounded) (Died later in the day) { 150327 Gr Hugo. F.	
	15th		31 Other Ranks posted to Brigades. RFA - 25th Div. Artillery -	
	19th		Move - 25 DAC - from S.12. & 7.7. (Sheet 28) to 7.2.d. 3.2 (Sheet 28)	
			Hd.Qrs - " - " - " - 4 " 7.2.d. 8.4 (")	
			No.1 Sec - " - " - " - " 7.8 & 6.8 (")	
			No.2 Sec - " - " - " - 6 " 7.8 & 8.8 (")	
			No.3 Sec - " - " - " -	
	21st		Lieutenant J. Blair - Invalided to England	
	20th		9 Other Ranks joined from RH & RFA Base Depot (Posted to DAC)	
	27th		1 Other Ranks wounded { 54332 Dr Holmes. L. (No.2 Sec)	
	28th		2 Other Ranks wounded { 76927 Dr. Pye. J. - (No.2 Sec) { 16036 " Killilea. J. (No.3 Sec)	
	30th		1 mule (killed) 2 mules (wounded) - all Shellfire	

In the Field - 30th June 1917 -

CS. Hype - Johnstone - Lt Colonel -
Comdg - 25th D.A.C.

Army Form C. 2118.

WAR DIARY or INTELLIGENCE SUMMARY

(Erase heading not required.)

25th Divl. Ammunition Column — Vol 2

Place	Date	Hour	Summary of Events and Information	Remarks and references to Appendices
In the Field	JULY 1917			
	1st		7 Other Ranks posted to TRENCH MORTARS – 25th DIVISION –	
	2nd		3 " " " "	
	4th		86 NCO's & men joined from BASE. (Posted as follows – (30. 110th Bde RFA)(29 – 112th Bde RFA)(27 – 25th DAC.)	
	5th		MOVE – from T.2 & 3.2 to G.21.a.	
	5th		2 H.D. Horses wounded by Shell fire. (one subsequently destroyed – 6–7–17)	
	10th		5 Other Ranks wounded by Shell fire. (one died of wounds)	
	12th		2 Horses & 2 Mules killed & 2 mules wounded by shell fire –	
	"		Other Ranks – 1 killed – 16 wounded (one subsequently died)	
	"		2 Horses & 14 Mules killed – 1 Horse & 14 Mules wounded – 1 Horse & 11 Mules missing (Believed Killed)	
	"		1.10th QF Wagon & 4. G.S. Wagons destroyed by Shell fire.	
	"		2. 18 Pr QF Wagons missing (one recovered 14/15th instants)	
	13th		28 Remounts received from BASE (L.D. Horses)	
	16th		1 Mule killed by Shell fire	
	17th		CASUALTIES – 1 Officer (Lt. M. Atkinson) & 6 Other Ranks wounded by Shell fire –	
	18th		1 Officer (Lt. W. Atkinson) & 2 Other Ranks wounded on 17th instant – died of wounds –	
	21st		5 Other Ranks posted to French Mortars – 25th Division –	
	22nd		13 Other Ranks posted to 110th Bde RFA – 12 Other Ranks posted to 112th Bde RFA –	
	27th		1 Other Rank wounded – 1 Other Rank passed – 1 Other Rank accidentally run over	
	"		27 Other Ranks joined from RH & RFA Depot (Base) – 18 posted to 110th Bde RFA – (28–7–17)	
			11 " " 112th Bde RFA (" –)	
			8 " " T.M. Group – 25th Division (" –)	
	29th		44 Remounts joined from Base (22 L.D. Horses)(22 Mules)	

O.S. Hope – Lt. Colonel
Comdg – 25th DAC –

31st July 1917 –

Army Form C. 2118.

25th DIVISIONAL AMMUNITION COLUMN.
WAR DIARY or INTELLIGENCE SUMMARY.
(Erase heading not required.)

Nr. AUGUST. 1917.

Vol 23

Place	Date AUGUST.	Hour	Summary of Events and Information	Remarks and references to Appendices
	1st 2nd		CASUALTIES — Nº 119135 Driver C.F. Ford } wounded — 81st Fd. rejoined 6.8.17. Nº 23161 Gunner J. Gardner }	
	2nd		POSTINGS. 39 ORs. under foreld from R.H. & R.F.A. Base Depot.	
	"		CASUALTIES. 1 Mule killed. 2 mules wounded (subsequently died) Lieut. J.R. Neale wounded.	
	3rd		POSTINGS. 15 ORs under posted to 110th Bde RFA — 26 ORs under posted to 112th Bde R.F.A.	
	"		MOVES. Nº 2 & Nº 1 Sec. moved from H.19.a.5.4. to G.18.c.5.2. (sheet 28)	
			Nº 2 Sec. & Nº 3. Sec. " " to G.18.c.5.5. (" ")	
	4th		CASUALTIES. 2 Mules wounded (not evacuated)	
	"		2nd Lt. J.R. Neale proceeded to England (wounded)	
	6th		Nº 63056 Driver J.W. Jackson } wounded — Nº 67252 S.S./Sh. J. Parson }	
	"		1 Mule killed - 1 mule wounded. 4 mules evacuated (sick)	
	8th		Nº 850 Gunner A.E. Cole — killed.	
	11th		4 Riding horses received from 225th Div. Coy.	
	"		CASUALTIES. Nº 119855 Driver Maand - killed - Nº 1032. Driver Andrews - } wounded - Nº 108775 Gunner Forest - }	
			5 Mules - killed -	
	12th		5 Riding horses returned from 77th Field Ambulance. 3 Light draught horses " " D.A.C.	
	16th		POSTINGS — 18 ORs under 1 offs proceeded from R.H. & R.F.A. Base Depot { 15 110th Bde RFA	
	18th		PACK TRANSPORT SECTION returned to respective echelons. { 2 112th " " } 25 Bar. { 1 T.M. Group.	
	21st		CASUALTIES. Nº 205682 Gunner F. Cruxs — wounded.	
	23rd		MOVES. 25th D.A.C. moved from G.18.B.6 to { H.Qrs. & Nº 1 Sec — J.14.a.1.1. } Sheet 27.- { Nº 2 Sec .... J.14.a.9.2. } { Nº 3 Sec .... J.14.c.2.3. }

Army Form C. 2118.

WAR DIARY
or
INTELLIGENCE SUMMARY.
(Erase heading not required.)

Instructions regarding War Diaries and Intelligence Summaries are contained in F. S. Regs., Part II. and the Staff Manual respectively. Title pages will be prepared in manuscript.

Place	Date	Hour	Summary of Events and Information	Remarks and references to Appendices
	Aug. 27th		POSTINGS — 2nd Lieut W. Graham } Posted to 110 Brigade.	
	"		" " G. Macdonald }	
	"		" Lt. W.M. Upton Joined on posting from Base	
	"		" One Shoeing-Smith " " " "	
	28th		25 Remounts received from Base.	
	"		COMMAND. Major E.B. Collen D.S.O. took over command of S.A.C. during absence on leave of Lt. Col. C.S. Hope-Johnstone.	
	30th		MOVES. HQ & No 1 Section from J14 A 11 sheet 27 to G 18 C sheet 28	
			No 2 Section - J14 A 92 " " " "	
			No 3 Section - J14 C 25 " " " "	
	"		POSTINGS. 3 N.C.Os posted to D/112 Bde R.F.A.	

Father Major R.F.A.
Cmdy 25th D. A.C.
21/8/17.

Army Form C. 2118.

25TH DIVL. AMMN. COLUMN — WAR DIARY or INTELLIGENCE SUMMARY.
SEPTEMBER 1917.

(Erase heading not required.)

Instructions regarding War Diaries and Intelligence Summaries are contained in F.S. Regs., Part II. and the Staff Manual respectively. Title pages will be prepared in manuscript.

Vol 24

Place	Date September	Hour	Summary of Events and Information	Remarks and references to Appendices
	2nd		3 Other Ranks joined from BASE – and Posted as follows:– 2. 110th Bde RFA – 1. 25th DAC –	
	4th		Invalided to England – Lieut. L. de Kelly MC.	
	5th		Riding Horse – received from Camp Commandant. 25th Division. –	
	6th		9. HORSES – received from 25th Divisional Train –	
	7th		23 Other Ranks joined from BASE – Posted $\left\{\begin{array}{l}5 - 110^{th} Bde RFA\\ 1. 112^{th} Bde RFA\\ 17. 25^{th} DAC\end{array}\right.$	
	7th		12 other Ranks posted to 110th Bde RFA.	
	9th		14 Other Ranks (Drivers) posted from No 1 RA. Reinforcements Cry –	
	9th		33 Other Ranks (gunners) posted from Base – posted to $\left\{\begin{array}{l}25 - 110^{th} Bde RFA\\ 8. 112^{th} Bde RFA\end{array}\right.$	
	10th		MOVE – from G.18 (Sheet 28) to EECKE Area – Ref. Map. S.A. Hazebrouck –	
	10th		CASUALTIES – No. 3. 77/128 B.T. R. Atherton (No 2 Sec.) + 204240 Bbr H. Booth (No 3 Sec.) Wounded – No. 2. 77/128 Dr. R. Atherton (Head & Forearm) on No 46 CCS	
	16th		MOVE – from EECKE Area to THIENNES – Reference. Map. S. A. Hazebrouck –	
	17th		" – from THIENNES to NEDON – " –	
	18th		Lieutenant R.S. Gillespie joined from Base –	
	19th		15 Other Ranks joined from Base –	
	20th		15 Other Ranks posted as follows. $\left\{\begin{array}{l}4. 110^{th} Bde RFA\\ 9. 112^{th} Bde RFA\end{array}\right.$ 21.9.17 –	
	24th		Lieutenant W.H. Taylor D.H. Thomson } joined from Base – Lieutenant W.F. Macrae	
	28th		2nd Lieutenant W.H. Taylor } posted to T.M. Group – Lieutenant W.F. Macrae	
	28th		REORGANIZATION – The following evacuated:– 1 Officer, 3 WOs, 18 Drivers. 36 L.D. Horses, 7 G.S. Wagons + 1 Maltese Cart.	
	30th		MOVE – from NEDON (Ref Map S.A. Hazebrouck) to SAINS-EN-GOHELLE (Rf Map 11. Lens) –	

September 30th 1917 –

C.S. Hyde. Johnstone. Lieut Colonel
Comdg. 25th Divl Ammn Column.

Army Form C. 2118.

Instructions regarding War Diaries and Intelligence Summaries are contained in F. S. Regs., Part II. and the Staff Manual respectively. Title pages will be prepared in manuscript.

WAR DIARY
or
INTELLIGENCE SUMMARY.

(Erase heading not required.)

(OCTOBER. 1st – 31st. 1917)   (25th = Divl. Amm. Column.)

9/01 25

Place	Date	Hour	Summary of Events and Information	Remarks and references to Appendices
	Oct. 17			
	3rd		12 OTHER RANKS sent to BASE. (Surplus n Reorganisation)	
	"		34 OTHER RANKS joined from BASE.	
	4th		2 OTHER RANKS joined from BASE. (Absent from draft on Oct. 3rd)	
	5th		10 DRIVERS posted to 110th Bde. RFA.	
			1 B.S.M. & 10 DRIVERS posted to 112th Bde. RFA.	
	7th		14 DRIVERS posted to 25 DAC. (Distribution of draft joined 3rd & 4th October)	
	8th		GARDEN DUMP – Aux Noulette (MajRef Sheet LENS. II) containing 22,015 rds A, 14,786 AX, & 7404 BX handed over to 61st DIVL ARTILLERY.	
			MOVES – 25th DAC moved from SAINS-EN-GOHELLE to:–	
			Hd.Qrs. W. 29. c. 81	Ref Map BETHUNE (Edition. 6.)
			No.1.Sec. W.18. d. 5?	
			No.2.Sec. W.18. a. 2.6.	
			S.A.A.Sec. F. 8. & 97.	
	9th		POSTINGS (officers) – 2 Lieut. J.W. Shannon } to 110th Bde RFA	
			– " – D.H. Thomson }	
			Lieut. H.J. Green }	
			2 Lieut. A.G. Standen } to 112th Bde RFA –	
			2 Lieut. J. D. Gray }	
			– " – R.S. Gillespie } T.M. Group – 25th Div.	
			OTHER RANKS – Postings – 14 Gunners to 110th Bde RFA.	
			6 " " " 112th " "	
	14th		MOVE – Hd. 2nd, 25 DAC – from W. 29. c. 81 to W. 23. c. 91. (Ref Map BETHUNE – Edition 6.)	
	– " –		POSTINGS (officers) – 2 Lieut. D.J. Roach posted to T.M. Group, 25th Div.	
	20th		3 SHOEING SMITHS and 1 SADDLER joined from BASE –	
	24th		POSTINGS & EXCHANGE – No. 947728 D. Pritchard. R. to 56th DAC – vice No. 947922 D. Newm. A.E. to 25th DAC –	
	OCTOBER. 31st/17			

C.S. Hope – Lieut.-Colonel
Comdg. 25th Div. Amm. Column.

Army Form C. 2118.

25TH D.A.C.   **WAR DIARY**   NOVEMBER 1917.

or

INTELLIGENCE SUMMARY.

(Erase heading not required.)

Vol 26

Place	Date 1917 NOV.	Hour	Summary of Events and Information	Remarks and references to Appendices
	1st	REMOUNTS —	47 Remounts arrived from BOULOGNE for 25th Div — Conductor 2/Lt Hayes - N° 2 Section —	
	3rd	OTHER RANKS —	2 Shoeing Smiths joined from Base —	
	"	EVACUATIONS —	3 L.D. horses evacuated —	
	6th	TRANSFER —	N° 956205 Gr Dixon W. posted from 236th Bde RFA in exchange for N° 405533 Gr Birtwell A.	
	9th	EVACUATIONS —	2 L.D. horses cast by D.D.V.S. 1st ARMY & sent to BASE for further training —	
	13th	OFFICERS —	2/Lieut N. Gooch joined — reporting from BASE —	
	14th	POSTINGS —	N° 158735 BSM. J. Beadsworth posted to 28th Battery RFA (17th Bde RFA) —	
	16th	REMOUNTS —	4 L.D. horses arrived from Base Remount Depot —	
	20th	CASUALTIES —	N° 66912 Dr Wellinott F.G. (Killed) N° 78503 Dr Abbotts W. (Killed) } Whilst attached to T.M. Grant — N° 190385 Gr Rees M. (Wounded)	
	23rd	OFFICERS —	Capt J. Miller & Capt (a/a) A. Flowers and 4 NCO's proceed to Indian Cav. Base Depot to undergo Course of Instruction — re tending to Indian troops —	
	24th	POSTINGS —	N° 944556 BSM. T. Roach - posted to N° 2 Sec. (from 121st Bde RFA)	
	28th	OTHER RANKS —	10 Gunners joined as reinforcements — from BASE Depot — (from 121st Bde RFA)	
	29th	MOVE —	SAA Section moved from Le Quesnoy (F.8 & 85) (Ref. 14/5 BETHUNE Contour Sheet) to Verdrel (W.26.d.3.2)	
	30th	REMOUNTS —	11 L.D. horses arrived from Base Depot.	

November 30th 1917 —

C.S. Hope John Stone
Lieut Colonel
Comdg. 25th D.A.C. —

25th Div'l Amm. Col'n WAR DIARY DECEMBER 1917
INTELLIGENCE SUMMARY
(Erase heading not required.)

Army Form C. 2118.

25 D A C   Vol 27

Place	Date 1917	Hour	Summary of Events and Information	Remarks and references to Appendices
	Dec. 1st		MOVE – H.Q. DAC – From W.23.C.91 (Sheet BETHUNE – Combined sheet) to Gonnehem (Sheet-France 36a)	
	2nd		" No.1 Section – " W.18.a.26 " " "	
			" No.2 Section – " W.18.d.58 " " "	
	2nd		REMOUNTS – 1 Rider + 3 L.D. mules received from No.1 Field Remount depôt	
	3rd		MOVES – (By railway) entraining at BETHUNE detraining at BOISLEUX au MONT.	
			H.Q. DAC and half of No.1 Section	
	4th		Half of No.1 Section	
			No.2 Section (less 1 G.S. wagon + 4 Amm. Wagons with horses)	
	5th		Remaining part of No.2 Section	
			SAA Section	
			After detraining – H.Q.DAC + Sections marched to Moyenneville (Map Ref. LENS.11)	
	8th		MOVES – H.Q. DAC + all sections – from Moyenneville to SAPIGNIES	
	11th		DUMPS – Haversack Dump (Gun Amm. Refilling Point) (Map Ref. I.1. 27.3. Sheet 57c) taken over from 3rd DAC	
	12th		" From Dump (near SAA Dump) commenced of Fremicourt Road (map ref. I.19.c.8.2. Sheet 57c) Completed 25th Dec.17.	
	24th		MOVE – No.2 Section from Sapignies to H.16.C.9.9. (Sheet 57c.)	
	31st		EVACUATIONS for month – Personnel – Officers – nil	
			OR's – 23	
			Animals – Horses – 2	
			Mules – 10	

December 31st 1917
In the Field.

C.S. Hope Johnstone Major
Comg. 25th DAC

JANUARY 1918   WAR DIARY   25th Div. Amm. Column.   Army Form C. 2118.

INTELLIGENCE SUMMARY

WD 28

Place	Date 1918 JANUARY	Hour	Summary of Events and Information	Remarks and references to Appendices
	2nd		MOVES – No 2 Section – from H.18.c.99 to H.17.t.2.3 (Sheet 57c.)	
	3rd		SAA Section " H.8.c.3.55 " H.16 c 99 (" ")	
	5th		REMOUNTS – 4 L.D. Mules received from 195th M.G. Coy.	
	16th		REINFORCEMENTS – 20 Drivers joined from Base Depot – posted to DAC.	
			– " – 2/Lt L.M.R Bull } " DAC.	
			{ 1 Bombardier } " " 110 Bde RFA	
			23 Gunners } " " 110 Bde RFA	
	20th		REMOUNTS – 6 L.D. Mules received from 25th Div Train	
	22nd		REINFORCEMENTS – 2/Lt A.St.J. Sedborn joined from Base Depot.	
	23rd		" – A.J.M. Melly " 17 DAC – 6. 110 Bde RFA	
			" – G.A.C. Perth "	
			" – 6 Drivers (Signallers) – posted to DAC.	
	27th		ESTABLISHMENT – Indian Personnel arrived under Capt A Flowers	
			2 Sikhs	
			2 Jats	
			4 Brahmins	
			110 Rajputs	
			3 Jillepore	
			___	
			121 – Total	
	28th		POSTINGS – 2/Lt A.J.M. Melly to 110 Bde RFA	
			EVACUATIONS for MONTH: Officers – 1 Horses – 2	
			O.R. 16 Mules – 7.	
	30th		MOVES – Hd Qrs DAC – from H.8.a.68 to H.17.a (sheet 57c)	
			No 1 Section – " "	
	31st			

C.S. Hope – Johnstone – Lt Colonel –
Comdg. 25 DAC –

Army Form C. 2118.

FEBRUARY 1918   WAR DIARY   25th Divl AMMN COLUMN

INTELLIGENCE SUMMARY.

(Erase heading not required.)

Vol 29

Place	Date 1918 FEB	Hour	Summary of Events and Information	Remarks and references to Appendices
	2nd		OFFICERS — 1Lieut Transtrum joined — on posting to 25th DAC	
	7th		REINFORCEMENTS — 31 Other Ranks joined from BASE and were posted as follows:— 110 Bde RFA — 13 112 Bde RFA — 23 25 DAC — 5 — 31	
	9th		POSTINGS — Captain E.S. Brittain posted from 'D' Battery 112th Bde. to Command S.A.A. Section —	
	14th		MOVES — Headquarters 25 DAC from H 17 a 2.3 — to — H 26 t Central No 1 Section — do — — do — No 2 Section — " — " H 36. t. 6.8 SAA Section — " — " H 33. t. 3.6	
	"		REINFORCEMENTS — 15 Other Ranks joined from BASE and were posted as follows:— 110 Bde RFA — 4 112 Bde RFA — 2 25 DAC — 8 T.M. Group — 1 — 15	
	18th		REINFORCEMENTS — 7 Other Ranks joined from BASE and were posted to 25 DAC — 29 Other Ranks (INDIANS – RAJPUTS) — " —	
	23rd		REMOUNTS — 24 Animals (5 HORSES & 19 MULES) received from Depot. Abbeville — & posted to 25 DAC —	
	23rd		OFFICERS — 2Lieuts. J. Narcombe and A.W. Swann joined from BASE & posted to 110 & 112 Bdes RFA —	
	27th		REINFORCEMENTS — 15 Other Ranks joined from BASE & posted as follows:— 110 Bde RFA — 11 112 Bde RFA — 4 — 15 5 Other Ranks (INDIANS – RAJPUTS) — " — & posted to 25 DAC	
			EVACUATIONS — (for month Feb.) Personnel — 11 Animals { HORSES 1 { MULES 7.	

In the Field   28th Feb. 1918 —

C.S. Hope-Johnstone Lieut Colonel
Comdg. 25th DAC —

MARCH WAR DIARY 1918. 25th Div. Amm. Col. R.F.A.

INTELLIGENCE SUMMARY.

Army Form C. 2118.

Place	Date (March)	Hour	Summary of Events and Information	Remarks and references to Appendices
	2nd		OFFICERS. Capt. & Adjt:- A. FLOWERS from H.Q. 25th D.A.C. posted to Command No 2. Section.	
			Capt. T. LYNCH relinquished Command of No 2. Section & proceeded to Base Depot 2/3/18	
			Lieut. F.D. BARNES from No 1 Section to H.Q. 25th D.A.C. as Adjutant.	
			2/E A.D. ROBERTSON joined from Base — posted to 112th Bde R.F.A.	
	7th		OFFICERS. 2/E E.C. STEARY joined from 25th Div. T.M. B'ys — posted to No 2. Section.	
	8th		REINFORCEMENTS. 15 other Ranks joined from Base and were posted as follows:-	
			5th Bde R.F.A. 8.	
	11th		REINFORCEMENTS. 9 other Ranks joined from Base and were posted { 25th D.A.C. 7. — 15.	
			to 25th D.A.C.	
	12th		POSTINGS. OTHER RANKS — 8 Gunners posted to 112th Bde R.F.A.	
	15th		REINFORCEMENTS. 11 other Ranks joined from Base and were posted as follows:-	
			H.Q.R.A. 1	
			3 110th Bde R.F.A.	
	17th		POSTINGS - OTHER RANKS — 6 Gunners posted as 7 Mess — 110th Bde R.F.A.	
			7 25th D.A.C. — 11.	
			112th Bde R.F.A. 5.	
	18th		OFFICERS. 2/L G.A.C. PETER posted to 110th Bde R.F.A. 6	
	21st		POSTINGS - OTHER RANKS — 2 Gunners & 14 Drivers posted to 112th Bde R.F.A.	

CONTINUED.

MARCH 1918. **WAR DIARY** 25th Divl Amm. Col. R.F.A. Army Form C. 2118.
or
INTELLIGENCE SUMMARY.
(Erase heading not required.)

Place	Date 1918	Hour	Summary of Events and Information	Remarks and references to Appendices
	22nd March		OFFICERS. Capt A. FLOWERS from No 2 Section posted to Command S.A.A. Section.	
			2nd Lieut J.C.H. RUSSELL ⎫	
			2nd Lieut R.H. COLLEY ⎬ Joined from Base - on posting to 25th D.A.C.	
			2nd Lieut E.W. CORMACK ⎭	
	24th		REINFORCEMENTS. 8 other ranks Joined from Base and were posted to 25th D.A.C.	
	25th		REINFORCEMENTS. Postings. Other ranks – 10 Gunners posted to 112th Bde. R.F.A.	
	27th		POSTINGS. OTHER RANKS – 12 Drivers posted to 112th Bde. R.F.A.	
	27th		POSTINGS. OTHER RANKS – 1 Gunner & 2 Drivers posted to 112th Bde. R.F.A.	
	23rd		MOVES. Column moved from AVESNES - lez - BAPAUME to IRLES.	
	24th		" " " " to HEBUTERNE. (K.K.4.5.9.)	
	26th		" " " " to GAUDIEMPRÉ. (D.2.c.9.2.)	
	"		" " " " to HUMBERCAMPS.	
	28th		" " " " to BUS-EN-ARTOIS – ACHEUX ROAD – (P.2.a.)	
	29th		" " " " to BUS-EN-ARTOIS (J.26.c.5.3)	
			EVACUATIONS – (for month of March) – Personnel – 10.	
			Animals – 4.	
	27th-28th		TRANSFERS – To 112th Bde. R.F.A. ⎧ 8 L.D. Horses ⎫ with harness and ⎧ 3 4.5 How. Wagons ⎫	
			⎨ 8 L.D. Mules ⎬ ⎨ 4 12.8 " ⎬	
			⎩ 6 L.D. Mules with harness ⎭	

C.S. Hope-Johnstone Lieut Colonel
Commanding 25th D.A.C.

In the Field – 31st March 1918.

25th Divisional Artillery

WAR DIARY

25th DIVISIONAL AMMUNITION COLUMN

APRIL 1 9 1 8

Army Form C. 2118.

WAR DIARY
or
INTELLIGENCE SUMMARY.
(Erase heading not required.)

25th Divisional Ammunition Column
R.F.A.
Vol 31

APRIL 1918.

Place	Date APRIL 1918	Hour	Summary of Events and Information	Remarks and references to Appendices
	2nd		REMOUNTS. 120 L.D. remounts arrived at PUCHEVILLERS from the Base –	{103 L.D. Horses. 17 L.D. Mules.
	3rd		HORSES. 96 L.D. Horses transferred from sections as follows – {H.Q. Bde R.F.A. 48. {112 Bde R.F.A. 48.
	4th		REMOUNTS. 25 Remount Riders arrived at PUCHEVILLERS from the Base and were allotted as under:- {110 Bde R.F.A. 7. {112 Bde R.F.A. 7. {25 D.A.C. 7.
	6th		MOVES. Column marched from BUS-les-ARTOIS to AMPLIER – Map Reference – LENS 11 – 1/10,000.
	9th		Column marched from AMPLIER to RAMECOURT. Map Reference – LENS 11 – 1/10,000.
	10th		Column marched from RAMECOURT to ST HILAIRE. Map Reference. HAZEBROUCK. S.A.
	11th		Column marched from ST HILAIRE to MORBECQUE area – Map Reference. HAZEBROUCK. S.A.
	12th		Column marched from MORBECQUE to ST JANS CAPPEL – MONT NOIR. M.F. HAZEBROUCK. S.A.
	12th		REINFORCEMENTS. LIEUT A.C. WHITCOMBE and 80 O.R's joined from the Base and were posted as under {170 O.R's to 110th & 112th Bdes R.F.A. {10 O.R's to 25th D.A.C. Lieut A.C. Whitcombe to 25th D.A.C.
	12th		MOVES. Column marched from ST JANS CAPPEL to BERTHEN– MONT DES CATS. M.F. HAZEBROUCK. S.A.
	13th		Column marched from BERTHEN to GODENAERSVELDE. M.F. HAZEBROUCK. S.A.
	14th		Column marched from GODENAERSVELDE to BOESCHEPE – M.F. HAZEBROUCK. S.A.
	15th		Column marched from BOESCHEPE to GODEWAERSVELDE. M.F. HAZEBROUCK. S.A.
	16th		Column marched from GODEWAERSVELDE to EECKE – M.F. HAZEBROUCK. S.A.
	17th		(Continued)

Army Form C. 2118.

(in)

WAR DIARY
or
INTELLIGENCE SUMMARY.

(Erase heading not required.)

APRIL 1918.

25th Divisional Ammunition Column. R.F.A.

Place	Date April 1918	Hour	Summary of Events and Information	Remarks and references to Appendices
	17th		MOVES. Column marched from EECKE to GODEWAERSVELDE - M.F. HAZEBROUCK. S.A.	
	17th		CASUALTIES. No 71316 Dr OPENSHAW J.W. wounded by enemy shell-fire.	
	18th		POSTINGS. 15 Other Ranks and 25 L.D. Horses posted to 112th Bde. R.F.A. to replace casualties.	
	20th		REINFORCEMENTS. Following officers joined from the Base. 2nd Lieut. F.G. RENT. 2nd Lieut. E.J. CURPHY.	
	21st		MOVES. Column marched from GODEWAERSVELDE area to EECKE area - M.F. HAZEBROUCK. S.A.	
	22nd		REINFORCEMENTS. Following officers joined from the Base - Lieut E.G. MURDOCK. Lieut W.R. JOHNSTON. 2/Lieut R. METTS. 2/Lieut C.F. BUTLER. 2/Lieut E.C. BRIGGS. 2/Lieut J. HALIFAX.	
	24th		OFFICERS. Lieut E.J. CURPHY posted to 110th Bde. R.F.A. 2Lieut F.G. RENT posted to 112th Bde. R.F.A. Lieut E.G. MURDOCK posted to 110th Bde. R.F.A. 2Lieut E.C. BRIGGS posted to 110th Bde. R.F.A. Lieut W.R. JOHNSTON posted to 112th Bde. R.F.A. Lieut C.F. BUTLER posted to 112th Bde. R.F.A.	
	25th		POSTINGS. 16 Other Ranks posted to T.M. Group - 25th Division to replace casualties.	
	26th			
	27th		REINFTS. The following reinments were collected from No 5. Base Remount Depot - CALAIS and were allotted as under:- 45. L.D. Horses. 110th Bde R.F.A. 6/ 45. L.D. Mules. 112th Bde R.F.A. 6/ 25th D.A.C. 12/ — 21/	
	28th		POSTINGS. 13 Other Ranks posted to T.M. Group 25th Division to replace casualties.	
	29th		WAR ESTABLISHMENT. Orders received to adopt W.E. No 818 (British and Indian personnel).	
	30th		WAR ESTABLISHMENT. W.E. No 818 (British & Indian Personnel) adopted, and allotting other ranks posted to Brigades. (A/Rks — 6 110 Bde. 20 O.R's — 112 Bde. 20 O.R's 112 Bde. (Continued.)	

Army Form C. 2118.

APRIL 1918.

WAR DIARY
or
INTELLIGENCE SUMMARY.
(Erase heading not required.)

25th Divisional Ammunition Column R.F.A.

Place	Date	Hour	Summary of Events and Information	Remarks and references to Appendices
In the field	30th April 1918		EVACUATIONS. The following evacuations (for the month of April) took place. { PERSONNEL - 27 other Ranks. ANIMALS - 11	

C.S. Hope-Johnstone
Lieut. Colonel R.F.A.
Commanding 25th Div. Amm. Col. R.F.A.

(1) 29 MAY 1918.

WAR DIARY 25th Div: Ammunition Column
or
INTELLIGENCE SUMMARY.

Army Form C. 2118.
R.F.A.
Vol 32

Place	Date	Hour	Summary of Events and Information	Remarks and references to Appendices
In the field	1st		REINFORCEMENTS. 88 O.R's joined from 2nd Army Artillery School and were posted as follows:— H.Q. 25th D.A.C. — 3; 1/B 254 R.F.A. 20; 2/B 274 R.F.A. 22; 25th D.A.C. 28	
	4th		REINFORCEMENTS. 12 O.R's joined from 2nd Army Artillery School and were posted to 25th T.M. Group.	
	6th		MOVES. 25th D.A.C. less S.A.A. Section marched from EECKE to BLARINGHEM.	
	9th		REMOUNTS. Received from REMOUNT DEPOT, ST OMER, 23 REMOUNTS.	
	10th		MOVES. 25th D.A.C. less S.A.A. Section (Mounted) at ARQUES – MAP REFERENCE – HAZEBROUCK S.A.	
	12th		25th D.A.C. less S.A.A. Section (Detained) at SERZY-SAVIGNY – Map Reference – SOISSONS 22. and marched to – H.Q. D.A.C. — CHAMERY. No 1 Section — VALLE DU BOIS. No 2 Section — VILLOME.	
	13th		H.Q. D.A.C. marched from CHAMERY to IGNY-ABBAYE. S.A.A. Section already at IGNY-ABBAYE. No 2 Section marched from VILLOME to Camp near COHAN.	
	14th		Postings. 24 O.R's posted to 25th T.M. Group.	
	23rd		Moves. H.Q. D.A.C. marched from COULONGES to BASLIEUX-les-FISMES. No 1 Section } marched from { VALLÉ DUBOIS } to ST MARIE CAMP – FISMES-BASLIEUX ROAD. No 2 Section } { COHAN } IGNY-ARRAYE S.A.A. Section	

Attached (11) MAY 1918. 25th D.I. Ammunition Column

Army Form C. 2118.

WAR DIARY
or
INTELLIGENCE SUMMARY

(Erase heading not required.)

R.F.A.

Place	Date 1918 MAY	Hour	Summary of Events and Information	Remarks and references to Appendices
In field	26		MOVES. No 1. Section marched from ST MARIE CAMP to CAMP - N.E. of MONTIGNY. No 2. Section marched from ST MARIE CAMP to BOURAVEOURT. S.A.A. Section marched from ST MARIE CAMP to ROMAIN.	
	27		RETIREMENT. H.Q. & A.C. withdrew to ÉRIGNY and attempted to advance on UNCHAIR but without success and retired to CAMP - South of SAVIGNY. No 2 Section retire on FROISSY - R. - PONSARD and YEZILLY. No 1 Section retire on UNCHAIR and ARCIS - R. PONSARD. S.A.A. Section retire on UNCHAIR and VENDEUIL. During this retirement of S.A.A. Section disaster overtook it at COURLANDON. When it fell into the hands of the enemy and only by considerable skill and courage and ? to ? without complete capture. The following casualties were caused.	LIEUT E.G. ATTENBOROUGH } missing believed 2/Lieut C.E.F. PLATT } prisoners - 2/Lieut W. JONES } O.R's Killed - missing believed prisoners 39. Wounded 3. Animals missing (though believed killed) 26. 3 missing believed captured - 107.
	28		RETIREMENT. H.Q. D.A.C. marched to AOUGNY and later withdrew to VILLARS-AGRON. 25 G.S. wagons & 14 limbers G.S. wagons fell in this retreat into the hands of the enemy. No 1. Section retired on ROMIGNY and CHATILLON. No 2. Section marched from YEZILLY to AOUGNY and later withdrew to VILLARS-AGRON. S.A.A. Section retired to AOUGNY and withdrew later to VILLARS-AGRON.	

Confidential (III) 25th Divl. Ammunition Column Army Form C. 2118.
MAY 1918.   R.F.A.

WAR DIARY
or
INTELLIGENCE SUMMARY.
(Erase heading not required.)

Place	Date 1918 May	Hour	Summary of Events and Information	Remarks and references to Appendices
In the Field	29th		RETIREMENT. H.Q. D.A.C. No 2. Section D.A.C. & S.A.A. Section D.A.C. marched to PASSY where a further order to withdraw was received when the Column retired on VERMEUIL and crossed the MARNE and camped just S. of SOUPMAYS.	
	30th		Further withdrawal was ordered when the Column marched to LA CHAPELLE. No 1 Section 25th D.A.C. rejoin the Column & marched from CHATILLON to LA CHAPELLE. H.Q. and all sections 25th D.A.C. march from LA CHAPELLE to LA VILLE-SOUS-ORBAIS.	
	31st		H.Q. and all sections 25th D.A.C. march from LAVILLE-SOUS-ORBAIS to MONT AMIS near BECQUEREL.	[MAP REFERENCES for all places. SOISSONS 32 - [French map] CHAZOYS 33 - [French map]]
	27th		ANIMALS. 49 animals were handed over to 112th Bde R.F.A. 14 animals killed by enemy shell fire. 107 animals missing (believed captured) - vide report - page 2	
In the Field				
31st May 1918.				

C.S. Hope-Johnstone
Lt-Colonel Commanding
25th Divl. Amm. Cal. R.F.A.

25

WAR DIARY or **INTELLIGENCE SUMMARY**
(Erase heading not required.)

Army Form C. 2118.

25th Divisional Amm: Column, R.F.A.

W 33

Place	Date	Hour	Summary of Events and Information	Remarks and references to Appendices
In the Field	June 1918			
	1st		POSTINGS – 7 Gunners posted to D/110th Bde R.F.A.	
	2nd		MOVES – 25th D.A.C. moved from MONT AMIS (near BERGÈRES) to CHATEAU DE LA GRAYELLE S. (Map Reference – CHALONS – French Sheet)	
	3rd		MOVES – No.2. Section moved into action under 19th Div: Arty at HAUTVILLERS Nr. N. of EPERNAY. to relieve a Section	
	4th		POSTINGS – 7/8th D.A.C. on Ammunition Supply. 9 Drivers and 18 Mules to A/112th Bde R.F.A.	
	5th		MOVES – H.Q. No.1. Section + details of No.2 + S.A.A. Sections move from CHATEAU DE LA GRAYELLES to OYES. (Chalons Sheet)	
	7th		MOVES – H.Q. No.1. Section + details of No.2 + S.A.A. Sections move from OYES to OGNES (CHALONS & ARCIS French maps)	
	21st		ANIMALS – All G.S. and 4-5. Horse ammunition wagons reduced in D.A.C. from 6 to 4 animals.	
	22nd		MOVES – No.2. Section rejoins the Column from detachment with 19th Div: Arty and marches to OGNES	
	23rd		MOVES – No.1. Section marches with No.6 Bde R.F.A. to ARCIS Railhead – ENTRAINED for HESDIN – 24-6-18.	
	24th		MOVES – No.2. Section marches with 112th Bde R.F.A. to SOMMESOUS Railhead – Entrained for HESDIN – 25-6-18.	
			MOVES – H.Q. D.A.C. marches to SOMMESOUS independently and entrained for HESDIN – 26-6-18.	
	28 & 29		DETRAINMENT – 25th D.A.C. on detraining Concentrate at EMBRAY – (Map reference – ABBEVILLE Sheet)	
	30th		MOVES – H.Q. No.1. No.2 & details of S.A.A. Sections march from EMBRAY to HAIL – 6 miles S.E. of HESDIN. (Map reference – LENS II.)	

C.S. Hope-Phustrie
Lieut-Colonel R.F.A.
Commanding 25th D.A.C.

Army Form C. 2118.

WAR DIARY
or
INTELLIGENCE SUMMARY

25th D.A.C. July 1918

Vol 34

Instructions regarding War Diaries and Intelligence Summaries are contained in F.S. Regs, Part II and the Staff Manual respectively. Title pages will be prepared in manuscript.

Place	Date	Hour	Summary of Events and Information	Remarks and references to Appendices
In the Field	1-7-18		MOVES. 25th D.A.C. march from HAIL to BARLY (Map Reference LENS.11.)	
	4-7-18		REINFORCEMENTS. 248 O.R's joined from BASE and posted as follows:— H.Q. R.A. 3. 110 Bde R.F.A. 117. 112 Bde R.F.A. 104. 25th D.A.C. 24.	
	5-7-18		POSTINGS. Cpl Skilling Smith posted to 298th Army F.A. Brigade R.F.A.	
	7-7-18		MOVES. H.Q. 25th D.A.C. & No.1 Section march from BARLY to ST LEGER-LES-AUTHIE (M. Ref. LENS.11.) OFFICERS. 2/Lt W.H.WATT 2/Lt E.THORPE 2/Lt J.A.TEES 2/Lt F.M.NORTON } join from BASE DEPOT.	
	8-7-18		REINFORCEMENTS. 59 Indian O.R's join 25th D.A.C. on the line of march.	
	9-7-18		MOVES. No.2 Section march from BARLY and join 25th D.A.C. at ST LEGER-LES-AUTHIE (M. Ref. LENS.11) POSTINGS. The following O.R's were posted from 25 D.A.C. as under 14 O.R's to 112 Bde R.F.A. 30 O.R's to 110 Bde R.F.A. 30 O.R's from 110 Bde R.F.A. posted to 25th D.A.C.	
			POSTINGS - INDIANS. 7 Drivers posted to 42nd Div. A.C. 4 Drivers posted to 57 Div. A.C. 58 Drivers posted to R.F.A. REINFORCEMENT CAMP - BULLENS.	
	10-7-18		OFFICERS. 2/Lt J.A.TEES posted to 110 Bde R.F.A. 2/Lt F.M. NORTON posted to 112 Bde R.F.A.	
	11-7-18		REINFORCEMENTS. Cpl Skilling Smith joined from BASE DEPOT.	
	12-7-18		OFFICERS. 2/Lt E.THORPE posted to 112 Bde R.F.A. 2/Lt R.MOSS posted from 112 Bde R.F.A.	
	14-7-18		REINFORCEMENTS. 2/Lt J.F.GILBERT and 10 O.R's joined from 3rd Army Reinforcement Camp.	
	15-7-18		DETAILS of S.A.A. Section (3 Officers - 130 O.R's) proceeded to BASE DEPOT to form a New Section with Third Army. 4/A/2454/18/Q/17/1/P.	

2353 Wt. W2544/1454 700,000 5/15 D.D.&L. A.D.S.S./Forms/C. 2118.

Army Form C. 2118.

WAR DIARY
or
INTELLIGENCE SUMMARY.
(Erase heading not required.)

25. 2 Divl. Ammunition Column.
R.F.A.

JULY – 1918.

Place	Date	Hour	Summary of Events and Information	Remarks and references to Appendices
In the Field	16.7.18		OFFICERS. 2/Lieut C.A. PELL-WOOLLEY joined from 3rd Army Reinforcement Camp.	
	19.7.18		2/Lieut S.B. ALLEN ″ ″ ″	
			2/Lieut C.A. PELL-WOOLLEY posted to 112 Bde. R.F.A.	
			2/Lieut S.B. ALLEN ″ ″ 112/2 Bde. R.F.A.	
	20.7.18		POSTINGS. 2 O.R's posted to 112/2 Bde. R.F.A.	
	21.7.18		REMOUNTS. 48 Remounts arrived from BASE and were distributed as follows:—	
			110 Bde R.F.A. – 25	
			112 Bde R.F.A. – 8	
			112/2 Bde R.F.A. – 3.	
			25 D.M. Signals. – 2	
			20 D.A.C. – 10.	
	22.7.18		REINFORCEMENTS. 4 O.R's } joined from Base Army Reinforcement Camp.	
			4 Signallers }	
			POSTINGS. 4 Signallers posted to 110 Bde R.F.A.	
	27.7.18		REINFORCEMENTS. 5 O.R's joined from Reinforcement Camp and were posted as follows:— 112 Bde R.F.A. – 2.O.R.'s	
			25 D.M. Sig's – 3. O.R's	
	28.7.18		MOVES. H.Q. D.A.C. No 1 & No 2 Sections march from ST LEGER-LES-AUTHIE to BEHENCOURT. (Maps Refs. LENS VI – ANISY(II))	
	29.7.18		MOVES. H.Q. No 1. No 2. Sections march from BEHENCOURT to MONTIGNY WOOD. (Maps Ref. Sheet 62.D. 1/40,000.)	

31—7—18.

A. Hope Smeeton
Lieut. Col. R.F.A.
Commanding 25. 2 D.A.C.

WAR DIARY or INTELLIGENCE SUMMARY

Army Form C. 2118

25th Div: Amm: Col: R.F.A.

Vol 35

August, 1918

Place	Date	Hour	Summary of Events and Information	Remarks and references to Appendices
In the Field	2-8-18		OFFICERS. 2/Lieut W.R. WATKINS joined on posting by War Office Authority.	
	4-8-18		OFFICERS. Lieut A. St JOHN SUSSORN rejoined from R.H. & R.F.A. BASE-DEPOT, LE HAVRE. 2/Lieut E.W. LUCAS (Gen: List) posted (to supervise the work of Indian Personnel.	
	6-8-18		REMOUNTS. 25 Remounts received from BASE and were distributed as follows — 112 Bty R.F.A. { 1 Rider. 11 L-Draught.} 113 Bty R.F.A. { 13 L-Draught.} 25th D.A.C. { 1 L-Draught.}	
	6-8-18		OFFICERS. Capt A. MEEKE posted as M.O. to 25th D.A.C. Capt C.M. DUNCAN joined from Base Depot. 2/Lieut F.E. TAYLOR joined from Base Depot.	
	7-8-18		OFFICERS. Capt C.M. DUNCAN } posted to 112 Bty R.F.A. 2/Lieut F.E. TAYLOR} 2/Lieut W.R. WATKINS posted to 112 Bty R.F.A. Major H. SEALY joined — and is attached to H.Q. 25th D.A.C.	
	9-8-18		CASUALTIES. 2/Lieut A. St JOHN SUSSORN (wounded) — and admitted into hospital. 2 Drivers (British) wounded — one invalid, 9th D.O.S of wounds — (9-8-18). 2 Drivers (Indian) wounded.	
	9-8-18		OFFICERS. Capt W. HAMILTON A.V.C. proceeded to England on July. Report to War Office. 2/Lieut L.A.C. DE VEULY A.V.C. proceeded to England — (evacuated to England) and struck off the strength accordingly (Authority D.A.P.O 9-8-18).	
	13-8-18		MOVES. H.Q. 25th D.A.C. moved from MONTIGNY to BEHENCOURT — FRANVILLERS Road – (Map Ref: C.20.D. sheet 62.D.) No.1. Section moved from MONTIGNY WOOD to FRANVILLERS (sheet 62.D — Map Ref: I.5 F.1.2.3) No.2. Section moved from MONTIGNY WOOD to B.12.C.9.X (sheet 62.D. Map Ref: C.5.a.5.5)	
	14-8-18		REINFORCEMENTS. 14 reinforcements arrived from Base and were posted as follows: — 112 Bty R.F.A { 1 O.R.} 113 Bty R.F.A. { 8 Drivers.} 25th D.A.C. { 5 Gunners.}	
	16-8-18		REINFORCEMENTS. 22 O.R's arrived from Base and were posted as follows: — 112 Bty R.F.A. { 2 Bombardiers, 7 Gunners, 3 Drivers.} 113 Bty R.F.A. { 4 Gunners.} 25th D.A.C. { 4 Drivers.} Continued	

Army Form C. 2118.

(Continued) (ii)

WAR DIARY
or
INTELLIGENCE SUMMARY
(Erase heading not required.)

25th Div: Amm: Col: R.F.A.

Place	Date	Hour	Summary of Events and Information	Remarks and references to Appendices
In the field	17.8.18.		OFFICERS. 2/Lieut B.M.WATT proceeds to Corps Reserve Dump for temporary duty. (Sheet 62.d.-Map Ref. B-30.c.6.)	
	19.8.18.		POSTINGS. 1 N.C.O. and 4 O.R's proceeds to ENGLAND for 6 months tour of duty at home. (Authority Sept/6/1:17 14.7.18)	
	20.8.18.		OFFICERS. Lieut M.WHITEFORD proceeds on probation for 1 month at No. 1 Base Remount Depot – ROUEN.	
	21.8.18.		REINFORCEMENTS. 3 Officers. } arrived from Base and were posted as follows:– H.Q. R.A. 1 Gunner. 25 O.R.'s – } 1/2 B.F.R.F.A. 3 Officers. 10 Gunners. 5 Drivers. 1/3 B.F.R.F.A. (Sheet 62-d.-Map Ref. D.26.a.3.9.) 25 D.A.C. (Sheet 62-d.-Map Ref. J.4.8.2.) 7 M. Gunners.	
	24.8.18.		MOVES. H.Q. D.A.C. moved from BEHENCOURT-FRANVILLERS Rd to RIBEMONT (Sheet 62.d.-Map Ref. D.26.a.3-9-) an No.1 Section moved from FRANVILLERS & MÉRICOURT-TREUX Rd (Sheet 62.d.-Map Ref. J.1.5-6-1.4.) No.2 Section moved from BAIZIEUX to MÉRICOURT-TREUX Rd (Sheet 62.d.-Map Ref. J.4.8.2.)	
	26.8.18.		POSTINGS. 2 Corporals and 3 Bombardiers posted from 25th D.A.C. to 25th T.M. Group.	
	27.8.18.		MOVES. HQ. 25th A.A.C. moved from RIBEMONT to VILLE-SUR-ANCRE – MÉRAULTE Rd (Sheet 62-d.-Map Ref. E.27.4.) No.1 Section " " " TREUX " (Sheet 62-d.-Map Ref. E.22.d.) No.2 Section " " " TREUX " (Sheet 62-d.-Map Ref. E.22.d.)	
	27.8.18.		REINFORCEMENTS. 2/Lieut H.S. NOCK } joined from Base Depôt at LE HAVRE. 2/Lieut G.P. SCRIVENER }	
	29.8.18.		MOVES. HQ. 25th D.A.C. moved from E.27.-a. Sheet-62.d. to F.17.6.9.2. Sheet- ALBERT. Combined. No.1 Section moved from E.22.d. Sheet. 62.d G.2. CARNOY-SUZANNE Rd. Sheet. ALBERT-Combined. Do.2 Section moved from E.22.d.-Sheet-62-d A.25-6.2.9 Sheet-ALBERT-combined.	
	30.8.18.		REINFORCEMENTS. 28 O.R's arrived from Base Depôt and were posted as follows:– 1 B.Q.M.S. 1/10 B.F.R.F.A. 2 Signallers 1/12 B.F.R.F.A. 1 Bombardier 5 Gunners 5 Gunners 2 Signallers 5 Drivers 5 Drivers	
	30.8.18.		OFFICERS. MAJOR H. SEALY assumed Command of 25th D.A.C. having absence on leave of Lieut Colonel C.S. Murphy JOHNSTONE- R.F.A.	

EVACUATIONS { British Personnel – 10 O.R's } Animals – 12.
Indian Personnel – 3 O.R's }

H. Sealy
Major R.F.A Commanding 25th D.A.C.

1-9-18

2353 Wt. W.2544/1454 700,000 5/15 D.D.&L. A.D.S.S./Forms/C.2118.

WAR DIARY

SEPTEMBER 1918
25th Divisional Ammunition Column R.F.A.
Army Form C. 2118.

INTELLIGENCE SUMMARY

Place	Date	Hour	Summary of Events and Information	Remarks and references to Appendices
Hq. field	1-9-18		REMOUNTS. 24 Remounts arrived at COR312 and were distributed as follows:- 110th Bde R.F.A. 9; 112th Bde R.F.A. 8; 25th D.A.C. 6.	
	2-9-18		MOVES. H.Q. 25th D.A.C. moved to HEM. [M.R. Sheet 62.c. H.7.a.4.5.] No 1. Section moved to HEM. [M.R. Sheet 62.c. H.7.b.6.8.] No 2. Section moved to HEM. [M.R. Sheet 62.c. H.19.a.9.8.]	
	3-9-18		REINFORCEMENTS. 22 Reinforcements received and posted to 112th Bde R.F.A.	
	5-9-18		REMOUNTS. 96 Remounts received from CORBIE and were distributed as follows:- 110th Bde R.F.A. 44; 112th Bde R.F.A. 44; 25th D.A.C. 8.	
	7-9-18		MOVES. H.Q. 25th D.A.C. moved to ALLAINES. [M.R. Sheet 62.c. I.4.a.40-95.] No 1 Section moved to ALLAINES. [M.R. Sheet 62.c. C.28.D.1-4.] No 2. Section moved to ALLAINES. [M.R. Sheet 62.c. C.28.D.0-5.]	
	9-9-18		CASUALTIES. The Camp of No1. Section bombed at 4.0.a.m. by hostile aircraft. 1.O.R. killed, 5.O.R's wounded. OPERATIONS. 25th D.A.C. attached as mobile reserve to 74th (Yeo) Division	
	12-9-18		REINFORCEMENTS. 31 reinforcements arrived from Base depot and were posted as follows:- 110th Bde R.F.A. 30 O.R's, 112th Bde R.F.A. 1 O.R.	
	13-9-18		OFFICERS. Lieut M.A. MURRAY joined from 108th Bde R.F.A. and posted to No 2. Section. 2/Lieut H.S. MOCK posted to 110th Bde R.F.A. 44 from No 2. Section.	
*	17-9-18		MOVES. No 1. Section moved to E.8.C.0.9. Sheet 62.C. No 2. Section moved to D.10.D.0.5. Sheet 62.c.	
*	15-9-18		OFFICERS. Lieut Colonel C.S. HOPE - JOHNSTONE returned from leave and resumed Command of 25th D.A.C.	
	19-9-18		REINFORCEMENTS. 47 Reinforcements received from Base Depôt and were posted as follows:- 112th Bde R.F.A. 34 O.R's; 25th D.A.C. - 13 O.R's.	
	24-9-18		REMOUNTS. 72 Remounts collected from PERONNE and were distributed as follows:- 110th Bde R.F.A. 40; 112th Bde R.F.A. 22; 25th D.A.C. 10.	
			(Continued).	

Army Form C. 2118.

WAR DIARY
or
INTELLIGENCE SUMMARY.

SEPTEMBER 1918.   25th Divisional Ammunition Column R.F.A.

(Erase heading not required.)

Place	Date	Hour	Summary of Events and Information	Remarks and references to Appendices
H.Q. Field	25-9-18		REINFORCEMENTS. 58 Reinforcements received and were posted as follows:— 11 to 'B' Sec. R.F.A., 22 to D.R., 12 to 'B' Sec. R.F.A., 2 to D.R., 2 to D.A.C., 10 to B.R.S.	
	26-9-18		MOVES. H.Q. 25th D.A.C. moved to D.21.A.9.5. Sheet 62.C.	
	28-9-18		OFFICERS. 2nd Lieut. J.H. SCATTERGOOD posted to 112th Bty. R.F.A. from No 2. Section.	
	29-9-18		MOVES. No 2. Section moved to E.21.6.0.8 Sheet 62.C.	
	30-9-18		S.A.A. Section at ST RIQUIER near ABBEVILLE with the remainder of 25th Division	
			EVACUATIONS. During the period 1.9.18 – 30.9.18 — 37 Other Ranks. 4 Animals. 2 Animals killed.	
			CASUALTIES. 16 personnel during the period 1.9.18 – 30.9.18 – 1 O.R. killed } BRITISH. 7 O.R. wounded. 1 O.R. wounded - Indian.	
			DECORATIONS. M.4790 Corporal MILLER C.W. awarded the Military Medal.	
	30-9-18		Col. Hope-Johnstone Lieut. Colonel. R.F.A. Commanding 25th Divi. Amm. Col. R.F.A.	

WAR DIARY or INTELLIGENCE SUMMARY

Army Form C. 2118.

25th Divisional Ammunition Column R.F.A.

Vol 3

14 November 1918.

Place	Date	Hour	Summary of Events and Information	Remarks and references to Appendices
In the Field	2nd		MOVES. H.Q. D.A.C. moved to LE CATEAU from P.25.d. Sheet 57.b. No 1. Section moved to MONTAY from P.26.6.40.00. Sheet 57.6. No 2. Section moved from HONNECHY to MONTAY. Sheet 57-b.	
	3rd		MOVES. No 1. Section moved from MONTAY to FONTAINE-AU-BOIS - Sheet 57-A. No 2. Section moved from MONTAY to FONTAINE-AU-BOIS - Sheet 57-A.	
	4th		MOVES. No 1. Section moved from FONTAINE-AU-BOIS to MAROILLES. Sheet 57-A. No 2. Section moved from FONTAINE-AU-BOIS to MARBAIX. Sheet 57-A. H.Q. D.A.C. moved from LE CATEAU to FONTAINE-AU-BOIS. Sheet 57-A.	
	5th		MOVES. H.Q. D.A.C. moved from FONTAINE-AU-BOIS to LE PRESEAU - E. of LANDRECIES. Sheet 57-A.	
	9th		MOVES. No 1. Section moved from MAROILLES to HAPPEGARBES - Sheet 57-A. No 2. Section moved from MARBAIX to HAPPEGARBES - Sheet 57-A.	
	10th		REINFORCEMENTS. 47 O.R.'s received from Base Depot and posted as under:- { No 2 Bde R.F.A. -- 10 O.R.'s { No 2/3 Bde R.F.A. -- 16 O.R.'s { 25th D.A.C. -- 21 O.R.'s	
	11th		MOVES. H.Q. D.A.C. moved from LE PRESEAU to LANDRECIES. Hostilities cease at 1100 hours - Armistice Signed at 500 hours.	
			REINFORCEMENTS. 46 O.R.'s received from Base Depot and posted as under:- { No 2 Bde R.F.A. -- 9 O.R.'s { No 2/3 Bde R.F.A. -- 16 O.R.'s { 25th D.A.C. -- 21 O.R.'s	
	14th		MOVES. H.Q. D.A.C. moved from LANDRECIES to ST RENIN - Sheet 57-B. No 1. Section moved from HAPPEGARBES to ST RENIN - Sheet 57-B. No 2. Section moved from HAPPEGARBES to ST RENIN. Sheet 57-B.	
	15th		REINFORCEMENTS. 20 O.R.'s received from Base Depot and posted as under:- 25th D.A.C. -- 20 O.R.'s	

CONTINUED.

Army Form C. 2118.

WAR DIARY
or
INTELLIGENCE SUMMARY.
(Erase heading not required.)

25th Divisional Ammunition Column, R.F.A.

NOVEMBER 1918.

Place	Date	Hour	Summary of Events and Information	Remarks and references to Appendices
In the Field	19th		MOVES. H.Q. D.A.C. moved from ST BENIN to BAZUEL - Sheet 57-B. No 1 Section moved from ST BENIN to BAZUEL Sheet 57-B. No 2 Section moved from ST BENIN to BAZUEL Sheet 57-B. S.A.A. Section moved from ST BENIN to BAZUEL Sheet 57-B.	
			REMOUNTS. 17 Remounts sent from 25th D.A.C. to 64th Division. 3 Remounts sent from 25th D.A.C. to 567th Army Troops Company.	
	21st		REMOUNTS. 86 remounts received from BOHAIN and were distributed between Brigades R.F.A. and 25th D.A.C. 25th D.A.C. attached and affiliated to 7th Infy Bde Group for Salvage Operations.	
			REMOUNTS. 40 remounts received from HENNECHY and were distributed between Brigades R.F.A and 25th A.A.C.	
	23rd		REINFORCEMENTS. 66 O.R's and 1 Officer received from Base Depot and were posted as under :— (110th Bde R.F.A. — 1 Officer 13 O.R's 112th Bde R.F.A. — 33 O.R's 25th D.A.C. — 11 O.R's 25th Trench Mortar Groups — 5 O.R's)	
	24th		REMOUNTS. 20 Remounts received from HENNECHY and were handed to Brigades R.F.A.	
	28th		REMOUNTS. 20 Remounts received from HENNECHY and were handed to Brigades R.F.A.	
	30th		MOVES. H.Q. D.A.C. and Sections moved from BAZUEL to QUIÉVY Sheet 57-C.	
			REINFORCEMENTS. 49 O.R's received from Base Depot and were posted as under :— (110th Bde R.F.A. — 15 O.R's 112th Bde R.F.A. — 10 O.R's 25th D.A.C. — 23 O.R's 25th T.M. Groups — 1 O.R)	
			DECORATIONS. No 8/18 B.S.M. STOREY. R. awarded the Military Medal. (authority XIII Corps R.O. S.R.O. 4261)	
			EVACUATIONS. O.R." 29. Animals 11- including 2 wounded. In Action (Animals Killed Animals Died Animals Destroyed)	

30-11-18

C.B.Hope Johnstone
Lieut Colonel R.F.A.
Commanding 25th D.A.C.

Army Form C. 2118.

WAR DIARY or INTELLIGENCE SUMMARY
December 1918 — 25th Divisional Ammunition Column RFA

WO 39

Place	Date	Hour	Summary of Events and Information	Remarks and references to Appendices
In the Field	3rd		REINFORCEMENTS.- 39 OR's from Base Depot and posted as under:- 17 - 110th Bde RFA 10 - 112th " 7 - T.M. Group 5 - 25 D.A.C.	
	4th		ROYAL VISIT. H.M. The King visited QUIEVY. All available troops assembled in the Area.	
	9th		MOVES. No.1 Section D.A.C. moved- from QUIEVY to BEAUVOIS.	
	31st		DEMOBILIZATION 77 OR's demobilized - made up as follows:- 75 Coalminers 2 Demobilizers + Pivotal men. EVACUATIONS during month of November:- 19 OR's 8 Animals (mules 2 los).	
			Jan 1st 1919 -	O/offic. Commanding 25th DAC RFA (Sm) - 25th ATC -

JANUARY, 1919.

WAR DIARY
or
INTELLIGENCE SUMMARY.
(Erase heading not required.)

Army Form C. 2118.

25th Divisional Ammunition Column R.F.A.

R.F.A.

Vol 40

Place	Date	Hour	Summary of Events and Information	Remarks and references to Appendices
In the Field	9-1-19		MOYES. S.A.A. Section moved from QUIÉVY to MECQ. [Map Reference - Sheet 57. S.W.]	
In the Field	12-1-19		MOYES. H.Q. 25th D.A.C. and No 2 Section moved from QUIÉVY to VENDEGIES-au-BOIS. [Map Reference - Sheet 57. B.]	
In the Field	31-1-19		Demobilization. 100 O.R's despatched to Dispersal Stations for demobilization in United Kingdom.
Officers. 2nd Lieut W.H. WATT proceeded to England for demobilization - as a pivotal officer - Coalminer.
Officers. Lieut. E.W. LUCAS. (A.R.O.) 2nd Lieut J.T.M. RUSSELL } proceeded to England as conducting officers for demobilization parties.	
In the Field	31-1-19		DEMOBILIZATION of ANIMALS. 30 Class "Y" horses despatched to XIII Corps Collecting Camp BEAUVOIS for staging to United Kingdom.	
In the Field	31-1-19		EVACUATIONS. Evacuations during January 1919 - O.R's — 15.
Horses - 1.	

31-1-19.

SAMUEL Capt. R.F.A.
Commanding, 25th Div: Amm: Col: R. F. A.

FEBRUARY 1919. WAR DIARY 25th Divisional Ammunition Army Form C. 2118.
or
INTELLIGENCE SUMMARY. Column R.F.A.

(Erase heading not required.)

Place	Date	Hour	Summary of Events and Information	Remarks and references to Appendices
R.Q. Field.	18-2-19		MOVES. H.Q. and No 2 Section move from VENDEGIES-AU-BOIS to ST AUBERT. S.A.A. Section moves from HECQ to ST AUBERT.	98L 47
"	22-2-19		MOVES. S.A.A. Section moves from ST AUBERT to MASNIERES - near CAMBRAI.	
"	26-2-19		OFFICERS. Captain D.G. TACON - struck off the strength pending demobilization having leave to U.K. (Authority – A.G. 47. 13/2/19.)	
"	28-2-19		DEMOBILIZATION. { 7 O.R's proceed to CAMBRAI en route for U.K. for Disposal. { 7 O.R's demobilized whilst on leave in U.K. (Authority - Part II Orders February.)	
"			DEMOBILIZATION of ANIMALS. { Horses ---- 49. { Mules ----- 253.	
"			EVACUATIONS during the month of February – { O.R's ---- 14. { Horses -- 2. { Mules --- 1.	

In the Field. ST AUBERT. February 28th 1919.

C.S.M. Grant Monnahan
Lieut. Colonel R.F.A.
Commanding 25th D.A.C.

Army Form C. 2118.

WAR DIARY
or
INTELLIGENCE SUMMARY.

(Erase heading not required.)

25th Divisional Ammunition Column R.F.A.

No 42

MARCH. 1919.

Instructions regarding War Diaries and Intelligence Summaries are contained in F. S. Regs., Part II. and the Staff Manual respectively. Title pages will be prepared in manuscript.

Place	Date	Hour	Summary of Events and Information	Remarks and references to Appendices
Little Field.	8-3-19.		MOVES. H.Q. and No 2. Section move from ST AUBERT to ESTOURMEL.	
	30-3-19.		MOVES. H.Q. and Z move from ESTOURMEL to CAMBRAI.	
	1-3-19 — 31-3-19.		DEMOBILIZATION during MARCH. 4.2.32 O.R's proceeded to CAMBRAI en route for U.K. for dispersal. 6 O.R's demobilized whilst on leave. (Authority Part II Orders March 19.	
	1-3-19 — 31-3-19.		DEMOBILIZATION of Animals. HORSES - 55. MULES - 203.	
	1-3-19 — 31-3-19.		EVACUATIONS. O.R's - 6. Horses - 1. Mules - 2.	

C. Hope-Johnstone
Lieut. Colonel R.F.A.
Commanding, 25th D.A.C.

www.ingramcontent.com/pod-product-compliance
Lightning Source LLC
Chambersburg PA
CBHW081435160426
43193CB00013B/2293